"We now recognize that grief is not about closure and moving on. In fact, keeping a healthy continuing bond with those we loved and lost is normal—and helpful. Allison Gilbert's *Passed and Present: Keeping Memories of Loved Ones Alive* offers a wonderful guide for sustaining that bond."

—DR. KENNETH DOKA, SENIOR CONSULTANT AT HOSPICE FOUNDATION OF AMERICA AND PAST PRESIDENT OF THE ASSOCIATION FOR DEATH EDUCATION AND COUNSELING

"I've been lucky to trace my roots with DNA testing. My ancestors are from Nigeria, Cameroon, and the Congo. I didn't know these details until recently, and the discovery has driven me to appreciate those I love and those I've lost even more. Most people don't know I lost my father when I was young. I wear his ring all the time. Allison Gilbert's *Passed and Present* is an important and timely book. Her creative ideas for remembering arrive at just the right moment in history, guiding millions of us who are yearning to recognize and pay tribute to our past."

—DON LEMON, ANCHOR, CNN TONIGHT WITH DON LEMON

"Allison Gilbert's *Passed and Present* poignantly urges us to recognize the importance of staying connected to loved ones who have died. Flying in the face of all the clichés out there about letting go, it wisely counsels us to remember mindfully and lovingly—and offers the tools to do so."

—MEGHAN O'ROURKE, AUTHOR OF *The Long Goodbye*

"There has never been a book like *Passed and Present*. Allison Gilbert's eloquent and inviting writing style provides readers with practical and meaningful suggestions for maintaining a continuing connection with loved ones. This is a book everyone, including those of us who work professionally with the bereaved, will read and recommend again and again."

—FREDDA WASSERMAN, CLINICAL DIRECTOR OF ADULT PROGRAMS AND EDUCATION, OUR HOUSE GRIEF SUPPORT CENTER

"Passed and Present isn't a book about grief, it's a celebration of our loved ones and of life itself. Allison Gilbert gives us Forget Me Nots—practical, useful, necessary tips for survivors of loss to preserve our memories and live a joyful life. A must for everyone who has suffered loss, which is everybody."

—ANN HOOD, BESTSELLING AUTHOR OF *Comfort: A Journey Through Grief*

"After a loved ███████████████████ ████████████ ████ e uncertainty— what to do v ████████████████████████████████████ , and all those important and ████████████████████████████████████ could have really used *Passed and Present*. In this simple and handy book, Allison Gilbert provides surprising opportunities for transforming would-be clutter into cherished keepsakes. This book will do for remembering what Marie Kondo has done for tidying up."

—CLAIRE BIDWELL SMITH, BESTSELLING AUTHOR OF
After This AND *The Rules of Inheritance*

"What a wonderful book! *Passed and Present* is an invaluable resource, a bona fide primer packed with all the ideas and habits we need for remembering loved ones. This is a book about loss, and also about celebration; about the past, the present, and a future that embraces happiness, the people we miss, and all they still mean to us."

—GRETCHEN RUBIN, *New York Times* BESTSELLING AUTHOR OF *Better Than Before,*
Happier at Home, AND *The Happiness Project*

"*Passed and Present* encourages us to remember in a whole new way. Allison Gilbert's sensible, no-nonsense approach provides so many fresh ideas that readers will find inspiration on every page."

—CHRISTINA BAKER KLINE, *New York Times* BESTSELLING AUTHOR OF *Orphan Train*

DISCARDED

"Perhaps no one who experiences a terrible loss needs to learn how to grieve. But perhaps everyone needs to learn how to create a memorial without creating an obsession. Allison Gilbert's thoughtful book meets a need that most of us might not have even realized was there."

—JACQUELYN MITCHARD, BESTSELLING AUTHOR OF *Two if by Sea* AND
The Deep End of the Ocean

"Allison Gilbert understands not only the need for remembrance but also the profound power of shared stories and mementos. In *Passed and Present* she offers a fresh—and most welcome— approach to salving grief and staying connected after loss."

—DAWN RAFFEL, BESTSELLING AUTHOR OF *The Secret Life of Objects*

Also by Allison Gilbert

Parentless Parents: How the Loss of Our Mothers and Fathers Impacts the Way We Raise Our Children

Always Too Soon: Voices of Support for Those Who Have Lost Both Parents

Covering Catastrophe: Broadcast Journalists Report September 11

PASSED AND PRESENT

KEEPING MEMORIES OF LOVED ONES ALIVE

ART BY
JENNIFER
ORKIN LEWIS

FOREWORD BY
HOPE
EDELMAN

Allison Gilbert

SEAL

PASSED
AND
PRESENT

"In a world that urges us to 'move on,' or 'put this behind you,' the bereaved often struggle with a common challenge: how to remember the people they can't imagine living without. With a wide range of creative and compelling suggestions and activities, from food to music and beyond, there's something in *Passed and Present* for everyone."

—DONNA SCHUURMAN, SENIOR DIRECTOR OF ADVOCACY & TRAINING, THE DOUGY CENTER FOR GRIEVING CHILDREN & FAMILIES

"How we remember those we love is as important as what we remember. Allison Gilbert offers creative, resonant ways to keep relationships alive in a positive way with those we love who are no longer here."

—ROSANNE CASH, FOUR-TIME GRAMMY AWARD-WINNING SINGER/SONGWRITER AND DAUGHTER OF JOHNNY CASH

"In *Passed and Present,* Allison Gilbert has given us a remarkable gift. By recognizing a newfound thirst for looking back, she leads us step by step in ways to honor our loved ones and rejoice in our ancestors. This book is necessary and simply wonderful!"

—BENILDE LITTLE, AUTHOR OF *Welcome to My Breakdown, Good Hair,* AND *Who Does She Think She Is?*

"I was 13 years old when my dad died. As his first born, I inherited all of his belongings but was clueless how to preserve them. I admit to dumping nearly everything in boxes. Thirty years later, *Passed and Present* has given me reason to open them and begin anew. Gilbert's book is so innovative that it blew my mind. It's more than just making mundane scrapbooks; her novel ideas include using digital technology to bring loved ones into our high tech world. My son will now have a crystal clear image of the grandpa he never knew. *Passed and Present* is a treasure."

—CHERYL WILLS, ANCHOR, NY 1 NEWS, AUTHOR OF *Die Free: A Heroic Family Tale* AND *The Emancipation of Grandpa Sandy Wills*

For your loved ones . . . and mine

ISBN 9781580056120

Names: Gilbert, Allison, author.
Title: Passed and present : keeping memories of loved ones alive / Allison Gilbert.
Description: Berkeley, California : Seal Press, [2015]
Identifiers: LCCN 2015040212 | ISBN 9781580056120
Subjects: LCSH: Bereavement. | Reminiscing. | Souvenirs (Keepsakes) | Memorialization.
Classification: LCC BF575.G7 G54 2015 | DDC 155.9/37--dc23
LC record available at http://lccn.loc.gov/2015040212

"We Remember Them," Sylvan Kamens and Jack Riemer, *New Mahzor* (1977–1978) published by The Prayer Book Press of Media Judaica.

Published by
Seal Press
A Member of the Perseus Books Group
1700 Fourth Street
Berkeley, California
Sealpress.com

Cover and interior art by Jennifer Orkin Lewis
Cover design by Jennifer Orkin Lewis
Interior design/layout by Kate Basart/Union Pageworks

Printed in the United States of America
Distributed by Publishers Group West

It's a happy life, but someone is missing.

It's a happy life, *and* someone is missing.

—ELIZABETH MCCRACKEN, *An Exact Replica of a Figment of My Imagination*

Contents

Foreword

The first time I read about the importance of preserving relationships with the deceased was in 1995, in psychologist Louise J. Kaplan's landmark book *No Voice Is Ever Wholly Lost*. Challenging the widely accepted model (at that time) of mourning as a process of slow and eventual detachment, Kaplan writes instead about the necessity of maintaining enduring bonds with our loved ones after they die. Mourning, she explains, is not about relinquishing our relationships with the deceased, but about finding appropriate ways to stay connected. To have ongoing dialogues and internal relationships with lost loved ones, she posits, is part of a healthy, normal mourning process. And to pretend those relationships do not endure, or to deny ourselve the opportunity to maintain them, is to cast ourselves adrift, bereft, severed om relationships that might otherwise have continued to sustain us.

Yes! I thought upon reading this. *Yes!*

I had lived thirty years by that time, and had been motherless for thirteen of them. My mother died of breast cancer when I was in high school, and like many families of the early 1980s, mine stopped talking about her, completely, after she died. Remembering her out loud, sharing stories, depicting her as the vibrant, healthy part of our family she had once been, was too painful a reminder of what we had lost. Yet silence did not destroy the inner connection I continued to have with her—it just made it more confusing. Thirteen years later, I still felt her as a strong presence surrounding me every day. I consulted her in my mind, often wondering as I made choices if she would have approved or disapproved. Not that I told anyone about this: such an admission, back then, might have been considered unsettling at best, and pathological at worst. For a long time, it made me feel as if something had gone terribly awry in my mourning process, as if I'd somehow done it "wrong."

Fortunately, our culture's attitude toward bereavement has come a long way in the past three decades. Those of us who study and write about the death of loved ones, and those affiliated with the hundreds of bereavement centers that have opened across the U.S., now understand that maintaining connections to our loved ones, and remembering them as the dynamic, complex, multi-dimensional individuals they once were, is a critical part of the mourning process. In the twenty-two years since *Motherless Daughters* was published, I've heard many thousands of stories about grief and recovery. And one correlation has appeared more frequently than any other: individuals who talk about a death soon after it occurs, who continue to honor the memories of their loved ones, who allow those people to remain present in their lives, almost always fare better emotionally over the long term than those who attempt to avoid those actions.

Yet, no book has offered such consolidated advice or direction for how to easily integrate lost loved ones into our daily lives. With *Passed and Present*, Allison Gilbert has created the first handbook of practical, accessible, and economical tips for survivors of loss. From guiding readers to helpful websites to walking them through craft projects that repurpose treasured heirlooms, from introducing holiday-specific activities to suggesting commemorative acts that can be performed at any time of the year, Gilbert's list of "Forget Me Nots" is both comprehensive and innovative. Sprinkled throughout the book are numerous gems, including some truly unobvious ideas. (Turning a loved one's signature into a necklace? Brilliant!)

Gilbert knows, from personal experience, the importance of actively remembering our loved ones, and of the strong impulse to celebrate their legacies moving forward. The antidote to forgetting is not simply remembering; it is in reinforcing those memories again and again and preserving them for posterity. By emphasizing commemoration over sadness, and preservation over relinquishment, *Passed and Present* can serve as a trusted companion on any individual journey toward wholeness and healing after a loved one dies.

—HOPE EDELMAN

Author of *Motherless Daughters* and *Motherless Mothers*

Note from the Illustrator

The afternoon Allison called me out of the blue to ask if I would be interested in illustrating this book, the opportunity was so appealing I didn't hesitate for a second. I lost my dad suddenly a few years ago. He was my go-to for advice, I treasured his biting sense of humor, and, well, I just really loved the way he cooked meatballs. His death left a gaping void, and I reacted by immediately putting some of his ashes in my garden. Knowing he'd be there whenever I tended my plants and flowers was enormously comforting to me. But as an artist, I looked for creative opportunities to celebrate and commune with his memory even more.

One of my greatest pleasures is using old black and white photographs to inspire new, colorful paintings. I allow myself to reimagine the people in the picture and the moment the image was taken—changing the setting, altering facial expressions, and sometimes even shifting the light. I have a closet full of pictures in my studio and I rummage through them pretty often. I tend to pull out the ones that have a fun story to tell, put on some music that fits my mood, grab my paints and brushes, and get to work.

The most recent photo-inspired piece I've done is of my dad at a party when he was a young man, perhaps in his early thirties. He's sitting on a wooden chair, leaning forward in conversation, his hands resting comfortably on his lap. A fireplace is on his right. My father looks healthy and completely serene. The painting reflects just one way I want to remember him, and I feel especially close to my father every time I recall creating it, and every time I look at it.

We all need to find outlets for remembering that make us feel happy and connected to the people we miss most. This book has beautiful ideas to help.

—JENNIFER ORKIN LEWIS

Introduction

This book is not about sadness and grieving. These pages are about happiness and remembering. It is possible to look forward, to live a rich and joyful life, while keeping the memory of loved ones alive. I'll show you how.

Being proactive is critical.

When someone we love dies, we usually benefit from being passive recipients of support. Between the rituals of burial and the recitation of certain prayers, between the wakes and shiva calls, the bereaved, and those who console them, know their role and take their place. But consider the vacuum that happens later. I've never met anyone who's completely stopped thinking about the person he or she loved; our memories flood in and out and wash over us at anticipated and unexpected times. Yet for the most part, a year after, five years later, fifteen—the outreach that once provided so much comfort is mostly gone. When it comes to keeping the memory of our loved ones alive, *that work is up to us.*

This book is necessary because remembering is so closely intertwined with healing. Therese A. Rando, author of the seminal *How to Go On Living When Someone You Love Dies* and clinical director of The Institute for the Study and Treatment of Loss, argues that a certain amount of looking back is vital to moving forward. She writes, "One of the problems in our society is that people fail to recognize the importance of a continued relationship with the person we have loved and lost. Many think that to deal with the loss you have to forget the person who has died." Rando lists four processes individuals must successfully navigate in order to be considered fully resolved in their grief. "Keeping your loved one 'alive'" is one of them.

Honoring past relationships has proven to have such significant restorative power that noted grief expert J. William Worden developed an entire bereavement-recovery theory about it. This concept, which is now viewed by many as the standard for grief counselors and therapists, is explored in his popular reference guide for professionals, *Grief Counseling and Grief Therapy: A Handbook for the Mental Health Practitioner*. In it, Worden coins the term "tasks of mourning." This concept not only includes remembering as a mandatory tenet, but also underscores the obligation of mourners to take control of the *process of remembering*. The mourner "needs to take action," he explains.

When I sat down with Worden for an interview in his home in Laguna Niguel, California, he told me why his "tasks" theory is so important: "Death makes you feel out of control. Being proactive makes you feel stronger. Taking steps to remember leads to empowerment, and feeling empowered is absolutely necessary for living a full, happy, and loving life."

In the nearly twenty years I've been researching and writing about loss, I've read many other influential works. I've also reviewed dozens of scholarly journal articles. Yet the more I learned, the more frustrated I became. Every source I consulted either didn't provide any specific guidelines for remembering, or failed to provide enough. Even the landmark book *Continuing Bonds: New Understandings of Grief*—a work, like Kaplan's *No Voice is Ever Wholly Lost*, that upended previous theories about grief, arguing the psychological benefits of staying connected to loved ones— doesn't fully address concrete strategies for remembering.

Passed and Present fills this remarkable void. To my knowledge it's the first of its kind. It's also the book I longed for after my mother and father died, one that would have helped me greatly.

Hundreds of people attended the memorial services for my parents. Both times, in those first awful days and weeks that followed, I never had to look far to tell or hear a story. But a few years after they were gone, opportunities for remembering popped up mostly during the holidays. The same was true over the years when I lost my aunt, uncle, and grandmother.

These experiences were isolating, made worse because I was confronted with so many questions most of my well-meaning friends couldn't answer. What should I do with all my parents' belongings—my mother's jewelry, her scarves, my father's massive assortment of neckties? And how about the nearly endless piles of inherited clutter—the random collections of loose papers, official documents, silverware, dishes, gardening tools, photo albums, VHS tapes, film reels, and 35mm slides? What should I keep? Where do I even start?

For years, I struggled. Not only with my parents' and other family members' belongings, but with *how* to talk about them and *when*. Outside Thanksgiving and other set occasions, I hesitated to bring them up in conversation. Anecdotes I told my children seemed heavy or forced, and I didn't want to make my friends uncomfortable. In some respects, because techniques for honoring and celebrating loved ones are seldom discussed, I felt lonelier at that later time than when my parents and other family members died. And now, after comparing my experience with my work with the bereaved, I realize this unspoken reality seems to hold true for many people—whether you're missing a spouse, friend, sibling, aunt, uncle, parent, or child.

Over time, I came to an important conclusion. Perhaps it should have been evident all along, but it was essential for me to recognize nonetheless: nobody is responsible for keeping my family's memory alive except me. My brother, stepmother, husband, and cousin are all powerful allies, but for my mother and father and other loved ones to continue enriching my life—and for my children to get to know their relatives—it would be up to me to integrate them slowly into our already full and busy routines.

So I still worked, and ran to my kids' basketball games. But I also made the time to gather my father's neckties and work with a shop to turn them into a quilt. Years later, with the help of a potter, I designed a one-of-a-kind dessert plate on which my grandmother's coffee cake recipe was printed. And whenever we ate Chinese food I made a point to tell our young children how much their grandmother had loved dumplings and moo shu pork too. Since my mother died before Jake and Lexi were born, these silly observances resonated with them, making their grandmother just a little more real. (My son and daughter are now teenagers, so the stories have improved and evolved as they've grown.) All of this took effort, but I noticed it was working; I felt closer to my parents, and my children were developing a stronger connection to their grandparents— even without having known them.

I was also happier. The more I incorporated memories into my year-round life—as opposed to sectioning them off to a particular time of year—the more I was able to embrace *every* part of me: the people who have *passed*, and all that's good and fulfilling in my *present*. This realization was exciting to me, and made me feel less alone. Gradually, I began to notice similar thinking in practice everywhere, just never in the same place.

Angelina Jolie wore her mother's ring when she married Brad Pitt. *Good Morning America* anchor Robin Roberts blows kisses to her parents before every broadcast. Katie Couric launched a cancer center in her husband's memory. Jennifer Hudson started a nonprofit following her mother, brother, and nephew's murders. Kathy Griffin wore Joan Rivers' fur coat on TV in celebration of their friendship. Cheryl Strayed, author of *Wild: From Lost to Found on the Pacific Crest Trail*, tweeted after the Academy Awards about the significance of her and Laura Dern's matching dresses: "With @LauraDern in #turquoise post #oscars in honor of my mom #lungcancer #LUNGFORCE." Rosanne Cash, now more than a decade after the death of her father, Johnny Cash, keeps one of his shirts hanging in her closet. And Arianna Huffington wrote about redefining success and staying connected to ourselves, in *Thrive: The Third Metric to Redefining Success and Creating a Life of Well-Being, Wisdom, and Wonder*, in large measure because her mother had long admonished her to be present.

"The last time my mother was upset with me," Huffington wrote after her mother's death, "was when she saw me talking with my children and opening my mail at the same time. She despised multitasking. She believed it was a way to miss life, to miss the gifts that come only when you give 100 percent of yourself to a task, a relationship, a moment." Huffington now tries to orient her schedule around creating more equilibrium—a direct tribute, she told me, to her mother.

These examples, and many others like them throughout this book, are important to me because they validate the urge to reflect. People have always done simple and innovative things to remember loved ones. But since the majority of strategies have never existed in one place, it's been difficult to learn *from them* or be inspired *by them*.

Until now.

Passed and Present is a simple, easy-to-use guide for discovering fun, creative, and inspiring ways to keep the memory of loved ones alive. It's an upbeat and imaginative handbook that can be used at any time of year—whether it's Christmas or a random Tuesday in June.

The chapters to follow explore strategies for remembering with eighty-five memory-preserving ideas called Forget Me Nots. Some involve planning and patience; others require hardly any effort at all. A few entail spending money; most cost nothing. My hope is that every Forget Me Not will gently stretch how you think about loss—that absence and presence can coexist, and that moving forward doesn't have to mean leaving your loved one behind.

What do I mean by that? I want to encourage you to consider objects and heirlooms differently: not just the smallest knickknacks and largest pieces of furniture, but all those items that frequently end up in attics and basements—ticket stubs, birth certificates, graduation announcements, passports, and marriage licenses. I want to introduce you to Meetups and workshops designed specifically to give memories a boost. And I want to convince you that remembering can be a cheerful and utterly satisfying social activity—both in person and online.

I developed some of the Forget Me Nots while writing *Parentless Parents: How the Loss of Our Mothers and Fathers Impacts the Way We Raise Our Children* and *Always Too Soon: Voices of Support for Those Who Have Lost Both Parents*; others were conceived after consulting with experts not usually tapped for this kind of research—jewelers, antique dealers, vintage clothing shop owners, upcyclers, and artists who work in various forms and media. I also received inspiration from writers and genealogists, photographers and scrapbookers, and I enthusiastically borrowed ideas from other countries and cultures. Focus groups were the source of numerous strategies, and one mind-bending concept came from a seasoned Hollywood prop artist. Readers, too, had invaluable suggestions, many eagerly passing along what's worked best for them.

But finding and sorting through these ideas wasn't enough. I vetted the workshops and tested every app and website. I worked with artists and used their crafts. Concepts that at first seemed promising were swiftly tossed if they failed to impress.

Most of the Forget Me Nots are divided into the first three sections of this book. Part One, "Repurpose with Purpose," presents ideas for transforming objects and heirlooms. These Forget Me Nots offer inspiration for repurposing photographs, jewelry, clothing, letters, recipes—virtually any inherited item or memento.

Part Two, "Use Technology," provides ideas that can be incorporated into your daily, digital life. These Forget Me Nots examine the myriad ways you can use computers, scanners, printers, apps, mobile devices, and websites to keep the memory of your loved one alive.

And, since talking about loved ones is generally accepted and expected in November and December, Part Three, "Not Just Holidays," offers opportunities for remembrance at other times of year—be that a loved one's birthday or anytime, day or night, when you feel that recognizable pull. The concepts here create moments for reflection when none likely existed before—ideas for celebrating the words your loved ones used to say, the music they loved, and the activities that once brought them, and possibly you too, the most joy. You'll also find tips for carving out private time for reflection, and for hosting a Memory Bash, a party 100 percent devoted to remembering *and* having a good time.

Part Four, "Monthly Guide," represents a dramatic shift in focus. Unlike the first sixty-four strategies, which can be used at any time of year, the dozen-plus Forget Me Nots in this section are designed with the calendar in mind. Yes, this book is decidedly about everyday possibilities for remembering, but I also recognize that Valentine's Day, Mother's Day, Thanksgiving, and other special times of year present unique and sometimes significant challenges—and opportunities.

Passed and Present concludes with Part Five, "Places to Go," an exploration of meaningful travel opportunities. Destinations lure you around the world—from Japan to Mexico, from The Bahamas to Israel—to cities and towns where reflecting and honoring loved ones is a communal activity. I call this notion Commemorative Travel. Following each location, I include a section called Bring it Home, offering additional sites to discover in the United States—as well as ways to incorporate aspects of meaningful foreign traditions into your practices at home or near where you live.

The Forget Me Nots presented here are by no means exhaustive, and I recognize that not every idea will appeal to every reader. You may not want to make a pillow out of a sentimental flannel shirt, or perhaps won't get excited about cooking or gardening—but learning about various ideas could inspire you with your own. Plus, the "perfect" idea for you may change over time. My greatest hope is that the entire collection serves as a reminder: that keeping the memory of your loved one alive can be done easily and at any time, and that doing so can bring enormous pleasure.

Death doesn't end our desire to have a relationship with our loved ones. The challenge is first knowing that we can ensure the longevity of the bonds that are important to us—and then knowing *how*. I offer you both.

1   *Repurpose with Purpose*

Loss brings a flurry of emotions and oftentimes an avalanche of papers, books, photographs, furniture, pots and pans, table linens, piles of clothing, and all kinds of jewelry. Rearranging objects or completely altering their context can be a game changer in how remembering makes us feel. Bit by bit, remembering *can* and *should* feel good.

Mementos become clutter when they no longer bring us pleasure. If possessions are burdensome, you frankly have two choices: Give yourself permission to get rid of them (don't worry, there are suggestions in the coming pages about how to do that meaningfully) or reimagine how they are used so they make you happy.

The Forget Me Nots in this section focus on transforming inherited objects. You can immortalize collectibles, create stunning objects out of teacups and plates, and preserve watches, toys, coins, and buttons in Family Fossils. You can do some of these projects by yourself, some with friends, others with the help of artists and craftspeople I've been fortunate to discover over the years. These Forget Me Nots underscore the brilliant possibilities when we look at objects just a little differently and give them a touch of TLC and whimsy.

1.

Preserve Memories in Perpetuity

National Geographic magazine ran an article not too long ago about scientists studying a new type of stone. The image in the accompanying photograph looked unlike anything I had ever seen—more bird's nest than chunk of rock. Blue, green, and red bits (of what, exactly?) were stuck to the face, pieces of wood jutted out in every direction, and a strip of what appeared to be plastic wrap protruded from the bottom.

The discovery was given a name: *plastiglomerate*, defined as a fossil-looking mass that forms when "plastic litter melts" and mixes with sand, basalt fragments, and other debris. Experts believe the stone could serve as a critical marker of time: the period when humankind began using plastics in massive quantities—and then throwing them away. Despite how glum the finding made me feel about the state of our environment, it also gave me goosebumps; I immediately saw the potential for creating a fossil-like structure that could showcase a loved one's smallest belongings—forever.

I took my concept to Hollywood prop artist Marc Fields. Fields is founder and president of The Compleat Sculptor in New York City, one of the world's largest sculpting supply companies. Clients include set designers and major museums across the United States. After several brainstorming sessions, he and I came up with the idea to build a Family Fossil.

Family Fossils are easy to make and can be used as paperweights or displayed on a mantel. All you need is a simple glass container and boxes of "fake water" solution—the kind used to hold artificial flowers in place.

The first step is to choose your nonpaper objects. (Pick carefully, because once the project is finished there's no going back.) Next, submerge buttons, coins, watches, plastic toys—nearly anything small and solid—into the clear mix. Pendants and charms, sewing needles and pins, even washers and screws work well. As the liquid hardens, the contents will be immobilized, suspended indefinitely to be appreciated from all sides.

To buy large quantities of artificial water mix for numerous Family Fossils, feel free to contact The Compleat Sculptor. I have found everyone there particularly helpful. Locate them here: www.sculpt.com.

2.

A Different Kind
of Scrapbook

Nobody has done more to stretch my understanding and appreciation of scrapbooks than Jessica Helfand, senior critic in graphic design at the Yale University School of Art and lecturer at Yale College. In her book *Scrapbooks: An American History*, Helfand examines more than two hundred scrapbooks and argues they represent an essential and authoritative form of "visual autobiography." And while the photos and ephemera she analyzed were used to create personal narratives, Helfand opened my eyes to considering the memory-preserving opportunities of making *biographical scrapbooks*—that is, a scrapbook *about* another person.

To create a biographical scrapbook, start by gathering snapshots of your loved one. Once you've collected the pictures, locate a few pieces of flat memorabilia that bring back positive memories—letters and ticket stubs are great for this purpose. Then, find images that put all those objects and photos into their historical context.

Adding period imagery also separates this project from a regular scrapbook. Dates in traditional scrapbooks are usually ancillary to the objects these albums contain; the year of a dance recital might be printed on a program, for example, but not highlighted anywhere else. By going out of your way to include these symbols, you're able to root your loved one in history, making his or her life and legacy more tangible. Pictures of significant moments (presidential elections), public figures (actors and athletes), and common household objects (popular appliances used during their lifetime) are examples of terrific scene setters.

A biographical scrapbook is gratifying to make. For one, it takes time, which means carving out specific moments of your day for remembering. And since it's a project that can be done with others, you can create shared opportunities for reminiscing as well.

3.

Fashion Unexpected Jewelry

My mother passed away before I got married. To honor her memory during the ceremony, I had a long strand of her pearls made into several smaller pieces—a bracelet for me, and a pair of earrings for each of my bridesmaids and maid of honor. Wearing the bracelet still makes me feel close to her. And my best friend from college recently told me over dinner, "Whenever I wear those earrings, I think of your mom." While the pearls keep my mother's memory alive, I've realized since then that meaningful jewelry doesn't have to be crafted from other jewelry.

In the hands of the right artist, virtually any keepsake can be transformed into a necklace, ring, or bracelet. Robert Dancik, an acclaimed jeweler based in Connecticut, creates one-of-a-kind pieces out of the most unusual objects: a book of matches, a word ripped from an old menu, guitar picks, gears from clocks, playing cards, even corks from wine bottles. Dancik hardly ever uses items whole—he embeds slivers of them into a lightweight artists' cement he invented and then shapes the material into whatever design he imagines before it hardens. "The material I use is symbolic of what I am trying to do for my clients," he told me. "By encasing precious objects in cement, I protect memories forever."

For example: when Dancik's father passed away, he made a pin out of a brown leather button from one of his blazers. He set the button in sterling silver and added to the middle an aquamarine to represent his father's love of the ocean.

Dancik works with clients across the globe. He can be found at: www.fauxbone.com/pages/Gallery.

4.

Assemble a Touchable Magic Box

If you've ever seen kids playing dress-up, you've observed how effortlessly hats and high heels morph into costumes. Essential to the transformative power of such a pastime is the simple collection of disparate objects in a single place set aside for discovery.

With this model in mind, place a dozen or so objects in a small box. You can use almost anything—bottle caps, eyeglasses, gloves, lockets, money clips, patches, and bookmarks. Encourage kids to rummage through it all, making sure to mention where the items came from or to whom they once belonged. Because such items *feel* like they should be off limits, kids will relish playing with them. It also gives you somewhere to put all those little items you can't bring yourself to part with.

5.

Cultivate a Shrine

The way we arrange objects at home is central to our overall happiness—so much so that it's the first concept author Gretchen Rubin explores in her bestselling book, *Happier at Home: Kiss More, Jump More, Abandon a Project, Read Samuel Johnson, and My Other Experiments in the Practice of Everyday Life*. Rubin offers her own apartment as a case study. While most of her possessions give her pleasure, she writes, to "glean *more* happiness" from them she'd have to display them differently.

In practice, this meant Rubin plucked various objects from around her apartment and grouped them in ways that heightened their importance. She called this cultivating a shrine.

> In a little-used cabinet in my kitchen, I came across the china pink flamingo that I'd taken as a keepsake from my grandparents' house after my grandmother died. An unlikely object, but I'd admired it so much as a child that it seemed like the thing I should keep. I took it down and set it on a bookshelf alongside the glass bluebird that my other grandmother had given me.
>
> As I looked at the two bird figurines, it struck me as poignant that my long relationship with my beloved grandparents could be embodied in a few small objects. But the power of objects doesn't depend on their volume; in fact, my memories were better evoked by a few carefully chosen items . . . That flamingo and that bluebird brought back my grandparents . . . I didn't need anything more.

A shrine is not a religious altar. You don't need a statue or candles. All that's required is a few objects that remind you of your loved one—a knickknack purchased on vacation, a decorative perfume bottle, a cherished photo—and a bookcase, small table, or perhaps a silver tray. You'll notice that objects that once seemed insignificant on their own become imbued with a deep sense of meaning once they're given a special place.

And assembling a shrine doesn't have to take a lot of time. "It only took me a few minutes to make," Rubin told me last August when we chatted about the undertaking on the phone. "The most challenging part is picking the objects. For a shrine to be a shrine, it must be highly curated."

The unanticipated upside of cultivating a shrine is the sense of freedom it provides. It's easier to let go of possessions that *don't* matter if we carefully, lovingly, and artfully draw attention to those that *do*.

6.

Buy
Shadow Boxes

When the new Whitney Museum of American Art opened in 2015, I loved seeing familiar pieces by Ad Reinhardt, Jackson Pollock, and Andy Warhol. But the works that struck me most weren't paintings at all—they were odd, often confounding, three-dimensional sculptures.

Known as *assemblage*, artists take nonartistic objects—bowling pins, dice, cast iron fry pans, even blades from circular saws—and manipulate them, simultaneously taking them out of context and preserving their original identity. As I admired these pieces, my own creative juices started to flow.

Shadow boxes, like an assemblage, also have the power to transform seemingly insignificant objects into works of art. Not only can they be used to draw attention to high-value curios, they're perfect showcases for objects that might otherwise never find a stage—a broken pocket watch, manicure scissors, a single measuring spoon.

If you're willing to go bigger, many retailers sell shadow box coffee tables. These can be large enough to hold violins and guitars.

7.

Shine a Light
on Collectibles

If your loved one was a collector, chances are you're now the caretaker of dozens, if not hundreds, of trinkets you don't have space to keep. One solution is giving them away (see Forget Me Nots #58 and #59 for ways to make that process less guilt-ridden). An equally compelling option is keeping a few pieces for display in a manner that fits *your* home and *your* needs.

Worth considering are fillable glass table lamps. The bases of both modern and country style lamps are hollow and can be filled with virtually anything that's fire-safe—such as shells, beach glass, marbles, or thimbles. And if you have multiple collections, the removable base allows you to change the display over time.

Giving yourself permission to weed through your loved one's collectibles accomplishes two distinct and complementary goals. First, it decreases the likelihood the items will become oppressive; and second, it increases the chances the collection will actually make you smile. Fillable glass lamps are a means to an end—they push you to cull a large number of objects and allow you literally to shine a light on the objects that remain.

8.

Turn Leaves and Seeds into Art

Oftentimes the mementos we want to preserve come from nature. Years before Sandee Hill's father died of a heart attack, she'd gotten into the habit of taking a few poppy seeds from his garden so one day she could replant them in hers. "I didn't have a garden at the time but knew when I did I'd want my dad's flowers," the Michigan mom told me. "That was the garden from my childhood. I'd collect seeds and scatter them around to fill in any empty patches. When I got older, I began saving a handful every year. He and I both loved the idea of his poppies growing in my garden someday."

It's been eight years since Hill's father passed away, and, despite an intermittent house hunt, she and her husband still don't have a garden. But until they do, the seeds remain stored away, out of sight, in a mason jar. Hill confided: "I get nervous about them. They won't last forever, and I really wanted my two youngest children who never met my dad to grow up seeing his flowers."

I told her I had an idea. Just a few weeks before our conversation, I went to a coffee shop in my neighborhood that regularly displays art by local artists. There were two paintings near the door that made me stop and stare—abstract acrylic paintings on watercolor paper, beautiful on their own, that were made even more spectacular to me because they incorporated five or six small, delicate, and carefully placed twigs. The paintings were of lemon trees—playful and gleefully out of proportion. My brain instantly spun with excitement: how great it would be to have a piece of art that uses materials from our natural surroundings—a leaf taken from a loved one's property? A stone picked up from his or her driveway?

To my delight, I discovered that the artist, Selene Smerling, works on commission. A few weeks later, Smerling and I sat outside the same coffee shop and discussed her work. Sipping an iced tea, she told me how the "objects that work best are largely flat—leaves, pine needles, a piece of bark, sand, flowers, twigs, pebbles—and no larger than eight inches in height or width." Smerling, who is also an art therapist by training, says her work is fueled by her clients' emotional investment. "I want to hear about their relationship to the objects they send me. I want to learn who their loved ones were, what was important to them, what made them special. Knowing these intimate details helps my creative process."

While Sandee Hill still holds out hope she'll create that garden of her dreams, in the meantime she plans to be in touch with Smerling. If you like, you can too.

You can reach Selene Smerling via her website: www.selenesmerling.com.

9.

Display Postcards
and Letters

There's something deeply stirring about holding a piece of paper your loved one touched—all those loopy letters, dots, and dashes transport us back to a time when we perhaps felt the most connected, the most loved.

Take letters and postcards out of storage and use them as a decorative centerpiece in your living room. Find a basket that's large enough to hold them all but still small enough that the collection isn't swallowed by lots of extra space.

These once-private notes are great conversation starters. And by leaving them in a place where they can be appreciated, you'll likely find yourself rereading and enjoying them, too.

10.

Give Fabrics
New Life

There is perhaps no greater example of upcycling than what Eileen Fisher has undertaken in the last seven years. The fashion giant launched Green Eileen in 2009, an environmental sustainability program that encourages customers to return their Eileen Fisher clothing in exchange for a modest payment. Dresses and tops in good condition are resold as recycled clothing, the proceeds supporting education and leadership training for women and girls. The too-worn garments are dismantled and used in workshops where participants are taught how fabrics can be repurposed into new "value" items. Workshops have explored using old clothes to make handwoven rugs, table runners, and Moroccan-style poufs.

I find Fisher's classes inspiring, as they thrust me into uncovering a multitude of opportunities for using fabric in non-traditional ways. There are countless projects you can undertake, by yourself or with help—if not from friends and family members, then from local crafts-people like seamstresses and tailors. T-shirts and jeans can be transformed into throw pillows and bean bags. Fleece jackets and sweatshirts can be made into cozy teddy bears. Other ideas are listed here. For more, please contact me (contact info provided below).

TOTES WITH TALES: Corduroy and other thick materials can be stitched into duffel bags, gym bags, and everyday totes with the help of Totes with Tales (www.toteswithtales.com), a one-woman boutique in New Hampshire.

Totes with Tales shop owner and longtime seamstress, Nancy Roy, a retired kindergarten teacher and community college professor, was working on three bags for three sisters when I caught up with her. A fourth sister, the oldest, had passed away several years before. Roy was carefully ripping apart the seams of that sister's favorite linen jackets and stitching them into carryalls. "These totes are beautiful and meaningful," she told me, "but it's even more important to me that they're practical. I want customers to carry their memories with them."

Roy also works with a lot of surprising materials, including shower curtains (great for diaper bags), bandanas, cloth napkins, placemats, and towels. She incorporates original zippers and buttons whenever possible, too.

WOOLEN COMFORTS: Marcie Chambers Cuff also approaches upcycling from the Eileen Fisher, eco-friendly point of view. In her craft project manifesto, *This Book Was a Tree: Ideas, Adventures, and Inspiration for Rediscovering the Natural World*, she takes readers on a journey infusing new life into old wool sweaters, leading the charge to morph them into hair ties, earmuffs, and cozy winter mittens. "The best thing about almost any upcycling project," she cheerfully observes, "is that the thing you

wind up with is significantly more amazing than the thing you start with."
You can also unravel sweaters and use the wool to knit comfy new scarves.

LOVE ROCKS: Fabric can also be repurposed to make poignant outdoor decorations. To do this, cut a piece of your loved one's garment in the shape of a heart and glue it to a smooth stone with craft adhesive. Crafters generally call these love rocks. These personalized stones can line the walkway of your home or be especially tender adornments for a garden. Note that, for love rocks to last outside, it's important to waterproof them with an outdoor acrylic sealer.

For additional ideas, please email me at allisongilbert@allisongilbert.com using "MORE FABRIC IDEAS" in the subject line.

11.

Tell Stories
One Stitch at a Time

Taking your loved one's clothing and turning it into a wall hanging can also be deeply affecting. Rebecca Ringquist, a seasoned mixed-media artist who considers embroidery "a way of drawing," is expert at this. She layers multiple strips of cloth and embellishes the fabric with hand-stitched illustrations, words, and phrases. Ringquist has also identified a remarkable method for transferring images—photographs, signatures, children's drawings—to fabric, fully integrating them as design elements.

Author of *Rebecca Ringquist's Embroidery Workshops: A Bend-the-Rules Primer*, Ringquist teaches wildly popular classes across the country. But besides her outstanding credentials and skills teaching beginners and advanced students alike, what makes Ringquist so extraordinary is her super-bubbly personality. She is simply delightful.

Ringquist dedicated *Embroidery Workshops* to her grandmother, who passed away while she was writing it. She also teaches courses online, and is currently developing a class focusing on memorializing loved ones. As she puts it: embroidery is the perfect medium to "tell our stories." Check her website (www.rebeccaringquist.com) for updates.

12.

Approach
Textiles Simply

The previous Forget Me Nots involve recasting clothing as newfound objects. That might be okay for casual pieces, but for items that carry more ceremonial or emotional weight, it might be comforting to follow an approach that retains more of the fabrics' original identity. One might:

- Frame a portion of a wedding dress or uniform.

- Honor a religious garment within a display case.

- Wrap a portion of a love-worn tablecloth around a large canvas and mount it on a wall.

- Place lighter fabrics (dress shirts, blouses, and scarves) into eye-catching circular frames by fitting them between the inner and outer rings of several embroidery hoops.

The above ideas encourage showing off and enjoying meaningful fabrics. Ultimately, though, I hope every fabric-minded Forget Me Not nudges you in the direction of letting go—giving yourself permission to enjoy sentimental pieces of cloth without the gnawing sensation you must keep them all, or use them as-is.

13.

Make Sculptures
From Reclaimed Materials

Bulky household objects can also be turned into cherished works of art. Cammie Metheny, who runs 106 Vintage Co., a "rescued goods" boutique in Coleridge, Nebraska, has transformed paintbrushes, gardening tools, and even wooden table legs into wonderfully unconventional sculptures.

The process is straightforward: a hole is drilled into the bottom of an object, and then a steel rod with an attached base is screwed in place. One sculpture works well on its own; a cluster makes a statement.

Metheny welcomes custom projects. You can find her on Facebook: www.facebook.com/106vintageco.

14.

Curate
a Gallery

I used to have three shoeboxes full of official documents. Each contained the paper trail of my parents' and grandparents' lives—my mother's freshman-year college ID, my father's last driver license, the joint passport issued to my paternal grandparents—but I never looked at them. They were hidden under generations of old mortgage records and car titles—papers I certainly didn't need but couldn't bring myself to throw away. The boxes were a dumping ground, and would have stayed that way but for a genealogy assignment at my son's school.

The project brought Jake and me to rummage through every box looking for his great grandfather's birth certificate, which we found after a joyless and time-consuming search. Soon after, I promised myself I'd do a major purge, keeping only those papers that made me happy or helped me tell a story.

As it turns out, documents make stately decorations. To create a cohesive look, I recommend framing marriage licenses, birth certificates, passports, enlistment records, and other military papers in like-colored mattes and frames. A collection that spans multiple generations often works best—no need to arrange documents in chronological order. And consider giving home addresses prominence, as these can be refreshing elements.

15.

Commission a
Memory-Keeper

Articles your loved ones ripped from magazines and newspapers can be poignant reminders of what was most important to them, but they can also feel onerous if not handled *purposefully*. To put excess papers to use, consider working with the Happy Badger, an artist named Tanya Monier who lives just north of New York City in a town called Sleepy Hollow.

Tanya Monier specializes in crafting Memory-Keepers, vintage cigar boxes she painstakingly decoupages with old clippings. Monier can work with virtually any kind of paper, including handwritten recipes. Crafted in 3-5 days depending on the size of the box, each Memory-Keeper can store just about anything—jewelry, photographs, wedding and graduation invitations.

To reach the Happy Badger in her studio, email her at tanyamonier@gmail.com.

16.

Manipulate
Film Reels

The Happy Badger (artist Tanya Monier noted earlier) also creates bowls and vases out of old 35mm-, 16mm-, and 8mm film. And as she's the only artist I've come across who does this, she's well worth a second mention.

The metamorphosis begins when Monier receives your film reels in the mail. She unspools the film and then rewraps it around a wooden or vintage object. Using shellac to hold the strands in place, the Badger constructs one-of-a-kind vessels that take on a brilliant blue, green, brown, gray, or purple luster. The final color depends on the shade of film stock.

17.

Reimagine
35mm Slides

You can do a lot with old slides; the trick is handling them such that light shines through them. Some of the best ideas I've come across use slides to create shades for floor and table lamps, sconces, and chandeliers. They're also a colorful option for making stained-glass window treatments and hanging door beads. (Instructions and how-to videos for these projects and more can be found online.)

There are also unexpected ways to use slides at social gatherings. One is using them to create nametags for a large-scale family reunion. To make these, place a white sticker behind each image to ensure the transparency is visible. Then attach a safety pin to the back with a little sticky putty. On the cardboard above the picture, write the name of the family member attending the reunion; on the bottom, print either the name of the relative in the image or the significance of where the image was taken. (For example, "Aunt Ronnie's house in New Mexico.")

You could also punch a hole in the corner of each slide, string a piece of ribbon through the opening, and use them as charms to identify wine and cocktail glasses.

18.

Make
a Frame

To increase the likelihood of children remembering why all those people in your photographs are important, spend an afternoon together
decorating a special frame.

How you embellish the frame depends on both the child's age and
his or her attention span. For younger kids, glitter and gems glued on an

inexpensive, unfinished wooden frame work well, while older children can likely handle the kind of inspired projects found in Joe Rhatigan's handsome book *The Decorated Frame: 45 Picture-Perfect Projects*. My favorite idea in that volume suggests affixing frames with hardware: door knobs, drawer pulls, and old-fashioned key holes. If you still have access to your loved one's home, these items might be especially lovely to salvage. You might also decorate the frame with old-timey objects like brooches, buckles—even the frames of eyeglasses.

Making a special frame is a fantastic activity for a Memory Bash (Forget Me Not #43) because the value of this project is in the creating as much as it is in what you create. According to James L. McGaugh, neurobiologist and author of *Memory and Emotion: The Making of Lasting Memories*, "emotionally significant events create stronger, longer-lasting memories." Decorating a frame with others has the potential for being just this kind of "emotionally significant" event. Over time, the memory of the time spent personalizing a frame will likely reinforce the significance of the person *being* framed.

19.

Create a
Memory Magnet

A 2013 CBS News poll identified just how much Americans love refrigerator magnets; 87 percent of respondents adorn their fridges with magnets that display everything from red and yellow alphabet letters to favorite vacation destinations and beer. According to Anthony Graesch, chair of the anthropology department at Connecticut College and coauthor of *Life at Home in the Twenty-First Century: 32 Families Open Their Doors*, "If you want to know a family, take a look at what's on their refrigerator, typically the largest appliance but also a major repository of family memory. Collections of photographs, calendars, class lists, soccer game schedules, and magnets provide insights into who we are and what's most important in our everyday life."

If you'd like to keep a loved one in the center of your everyday life, you can easily create Memory Magnets using small family photos, epoxy stickers, and magnetic sheets. (The latter two are widely available online and in craft stores.)

First, affix the epoxy stickers (sticky-side down) to the top of your picture, giving it a glasslike finish. Next, cut a piece of magnetic strip to the size and shape of your sticker and place it on the back. Done! In less than five minutes, you've made a Memory Magnet you can appreciate every day.

20.

Destroy
Your Dishes

When was the last time you served dinner on your family's formal dishes? If you can't remember, these ideas may be perfect for you.

Carefully break a few bowls and plates. Use the bits of porcelain to create a mosaic for a serving tray or trivet. The tiniest pieces can be used as charms for a bracelet.

Would you prefer something more unusual? In her shop near Brighton, England, accessory designer Abigail Mary Rose Clark turns teacups into bangle bracelets sized for the wearer's wrist. Clark warns, though, that she's only able to use the strongest china. "The cups need to be in very good condition with no chips or cracks in order to survive the cutting process," she says. (For information on the best-suited teacups, visit her website: www.staygoldmaryrose.com.)

Of course, many people can't bring themselves to intentionally break their family's china. If that's where you find yourself, choose a few pieces to hang on a wall. Or if you like to entertain, build a three-tiered cake stand using your prettiest plates.

The bottom line: you don't have to eat on dishes to enjoy them.

21.

Share
Objects Broadly

The goal of every Forget Me Not so far has been to derive enjoyment from objects *at home*. This Forget Me Not takes a markedly different approach: to make possessions conduits of remembrance with people who may never set foot inside your house or apartment.

Liz Glasgow took this concept and made a career of it. Her mother, Hilda, drew fashion illustrations for some of the most popular national magazines and department stores. After she died, Glasgow sorted through sixty years' worth of her mother's drawings, papers, and art supplies and decided to keep her mother's memory alive by sharing her work. Glasgow now runs a company selling invitations, wallpaper, and gift tags adorned with her mother's designs.

Of course, you don't have to start a business to share treasured objects. There are simpler ways to increase our engagement with meaningful objects and commemorate those we miss. For example, a photograph of a favorite possession could be the focal point for notecards and other stationery. And the trick to creating dynamite stationery: taking a really good picture.

Robert Tardio, a commercial photographer in New York City who shoots product advertisements for Clinique, Coach, and other high-end clients, offers a few guidelines for photographing objects at home:

- Shoot on a cloudy day. Shadows will be softer.
- Place the object by a window. Natural light is all you need.
- Use a plain, white background. This can be a bed sheet or a piece of paper. White reflects light and gives more depth to your object. Patterns of any kind will be distracting.

But before you crop your captured image, Tardio recommends—to my surprise—manipulating the image so it doesn't look like a photo at all. "You could play around with an image so the object looks like a line drawing or some other kind of illustration. There's no need to be so literal. I love the idea of having a cherished object become a symbol of a person or time in your life. It makes the final result a little different, perhaps a bit more of a conversation piece."

No matter how you do it, recasting objects as stationery has another benefit, this one equally valuable. If the object is meaningful to you but something you'd rather not keep, immortalizing it on paper offers the *pleasure of the object* without the *burden of keeping it*.

22.

Repurpose Books

Our attachment to books frequently extends beyond the stories they tell. Underlined passages and dog-eared pages reveal our loved one's likes and dislikes—as well as the words and passages that resonated with them most. Books are also precious because we tend to associate them with special moments and places.

There may be plenty of books you choose to keep intact, but if you're willing to go a few unconventional routes, hardcovers can be given new life well beyond the bookshelf. For example:

- A sharp utility knife can turn book covers into mattes for mounting photographs.

- The cavity of a hollowed-out book can become a hidden safe or even an unexpected gift box, where the "box" is as much a gift as its contents.

- Books can also be made into purses and evening clutches, or their covers can become cases for E-readers, tablets, and iPads.

Some of the artists I've worked with in repurposing books include Michelle Wolett (www.chicklitdesigns.com), Karen Higham (www.etsy.com/shop/novelcreations), and Kathleen Scranton (www.beezbyscranton.com). Depending on what you do with your book, it might be possible to get your original pages rebound and returned as a paperback—just be sure to ask in advance.

Scranton's Memory Box is worth special attention. Unlike the Happy Badger's Memory-Keeper (Forget Me Not #15), Scranton's boxes are lined with quilting cotton (selected by the customer); she also exquisitely handcrafts each with archival materials, ensuring they last longer than if they'd been left untouched.

23.

Reconsider
Your Reflection

Look at yourself in a mirror. What grabs your attention first?

Make-up icon Bobbi Brown hopes you see more than any perceived flaw or imperfection. In the book *About Face: Women Write About What They See When They Look in the Mirror*, Brown states: "A mirror can and should be a tool that empowers you." To Brown, this means embracing your reflection and applying cosmetics to enhance "what is naturally unique, and therefore beautiful, in every woman."

I adore this notion. I'm also convinced empowerment can stem from using a mirror to build a deeper connection to the past.

To draw strength from family, surround a mirror with photographs of your relatives and ancestors—and then compare their features against your own. Notice the physical traits you have in common—the shape of your eyes, the curve or angle of your nose, the color of your skin. When writer Kym Ragusa gazed at her reflection for her essay in *About Face*, she saw her mother and every relative who "traveled an ocean" and "came together to make me." What do you see?

You can decorate a mirror by inserting photos around the perimeter or permanently affixing photocopies with specialty glue and sealer. Either way, you'll be adding your reflection to a personal and stirring mosaic every time you look in its direction.

2. *Use Technology*

Technology is the low-hanging fruit of memory-keeping. Emails, texts, and apps allow us to work virtually and socialize remotely. The power of these devices can easily be harnessed to keep your loved one's memory alive. The tools are already in your pocket and on your desk.

The Forget Me Nots here will enable you to remember in a contemporary context. By incorporating memories into your digital life, a dual opportunity exists to reflect *and* receive: You can share memories while simultaneously taking comfort in the stories and support that ricochet back. This symbiotic relationship is historic. It makes your loved one forever relevant and accessible, especially important if you're trying to get teens and tweens to remember as well.

On the following pages, each Forget Me Not suggests an opportunity for using technology. All share a common goal: encouraging you to integrate your loved one into the rich and varied digital life you already lead—whether at home, at work, or on the go.

24.

Get the White
Glove Treatment

If you've ever been to a party where the goal was hanging out with neighbors while buying kitchen gadgets, you have a pretty good idea how Legacy Republic works. This new memory-preserving concept, conceived by one of the largest film transfer companies in the United

States, had only been in place six months when I put it to the test with the help of an enthusiastic focus group.

A Legacy Republic representative comes to your home to make one-stop shopping out of digitizing film, video, photos, slides, even entire scrapbooks and albums. The transfer doesn't happen in your living room, of course: the consultant walks participants through the process, packages up their pictures and other media, and sends them to its facilities in California or Georgia. I found the process entertaining and casual—friends got to eat and hang out while the adviser peeled us off one by one to discuss our options and place our order.

Three weeks after my gathering, I was thrilled by how easily I could watch and share my video. In addition to sending the original material back in the mail along with a DVD, Legacy Republic provided a link to a private online account where all my information is stored. I can log in, drag my cursor to a section of video I like, mark beginning and end points, and upload the snippet directly to Facebook. Other participants were equally delighted with the results.

You can learn more at the company's website: www.legacyrepublic.com.

25.

Show
& Tales

Show & Tales unfold as "show and tells" did in kindergarten, except this grown-up version includes snacks and alcohol and is organized primarily through social media and Meetups. Themes for each evening are publicized in advance, and men and women are encouraged to bring a related object and tell its story. Topics have included dolls, cards, love letters, and thank you notes.

Organizer Martie McNabb started this outfit in Brooklyn. I attended a Show & Tale located in a sexy, candlelit Lower Manhattan watering hole, joining a small group sitting on red velvet couches and chairs in the back of the bar. Following the theme for the evening—The Family Jewels—people who'd never met before took turns describing what they brought and responding to questions. One woman who looked to be in her early twenties pulled a chain from underneath her shirt. From it dangled a high school graduation ring, her brother's. The group leaned in, listening even more intently, learning from her tale that he'd died a few weeks earlier in a car accident. And it was in that heartbreaking moment that the power of McNabb's gathering became abundantly clear to me: we may have been strangers, but to some extent we understood each other better, perhaps, than did our dearest friends who haven't experienced such loss.

Check out McNabb's Meetup page for locations and times: www.meetup.com/Show-and-Tales.

26.

Recall and Preserve
Their Voice

After giving a talk at a conference in 2015 I had a conversation with a woman about her husband, who had died a decade earlier. She was quick to remember the wonderful sons they'd raised, the beach vacations they'd taken, and the movies they'd enjoyed (classics, new releases, nothing scary). What struck me most was how happy these memories seemed to make her—until they didn't. At one point, her voice got stuck and dropped to a whisper. "I can't always hear his voice," she told me, as if admitting she'd done something shameful.

I understood her confession all too well. Inability to conjure a loved one's voice can frequently be a source of sadness. If you're fortunate enough to have old home movies or cell phone videos that have captured that voice, the following concept can make that audio recording more accessible. (*But even if you don't have recordings, don't skip this Forget Me Not. You'll find guidance for you here as well.*)

If you have old home movies, depending on the year the footage was shot, it's possible you have sound of your loved one talking, laughing, or singing. If so, and if it's not already in digital form, you can digitize the video and then edit its audio. What can you do with those clips?

You can use a few moments as a ringtone for your smartphone. You could also record one or two seconds onto an electronic paperweight, the kind available at most stationery stores. Both methods offer easy and frequent reminders of your loved one's voice. If you're lucky to have hours and hours of recordings, it may be possible in the not-too-distant future to create a cloned version of that voice—which could then narrate a passage from a book or tell a family story.

Audio engineers already manufacture computer-generated voices to help individuals with ALS communicate after reduced muscle function makes it impossible for them to form words. Before they lose the ability to speak, patients recite and record dozens of specially written sentences into a web-based voice recorder. These recordings enable a new voice to be created that mimics their exact inflections and speaking patterns.

But what if you don't have recordings? Neuroscientist Anthony Wagner, director of the Stanford Memory Laboratory at Stanford University, says individuals can increase the likelihood of remembering their loved one's voice by directing their attention inward and focusing on memories with specific environmental cues. Wagner calls this "strategic recall." As he explained to me, "Memories are the product of our brain's associative network. If we're able to retrieve a memory of a place where we heard our loved one speak, or recall an event closely associated with that individual, additional memories will come to mind, and some of them might be the sound of his or her voice."

The trick, Wagner insists, is to minimize external distractions when trying to summon up a loved one's particular tones and intonations. A "generous amount" of uninterrupted time is more likely to "unlock" a voice from your memory bank than will repeated, cursory attempts.

27.

Invite
Comments

Although it's certainly a distinction she'd prefer not to have, Alexandra Zaslow is a role model for harnessing the power of technology as a means for keeping the memory of loved ones alive. In 2012 she lost her father, famed writer Jeffrey Zaslow (coauthor of the runaway bestsellers *The Last Lecture* and *Highest Duty*) in a car accident. He'd been on tour for his latest book, *The Magic Room*, when he lost control of his car on a snow-covered road in northern Michigan.

Almost immediately after his death Zaslow turned to her friends online. "Being able to post is the best way I know to make sure my dad is never forgotten," she told me. "He was my everything."

Zaslow posts about her dad on his birthday, Father's Day, and when there's a story in the news she thinks he'd have an opinion on. The posts show up on my Facebook feed not because I'm "Friends" with Zaslow, but because I was "Friends" with her father. She and her sisters keep his Facebook page active and tag him with every update, with posts like:

> Thinking of my dad today on the 3 year anniversary and how much I miss him. I'd love if everyone can remember him with me today and share their favorite memory in the comments.

I was gobsmacked by this post. Zaslow didn't just inform—she proactively asked her friends *and her father's friends* to share their memories too. Zaslow's request resulted in 481 "Likes" and 130 comments, an ocean of virtual story sharing from relatives, neighbors, friends, colleagues, and coworkers.

To follow are what I consider the most valuable lessons from Zaslow's story.

On the anniversary of your loved one's death, update your Facebook status by requesting friends share a favorite memory. Also on the anniversary, temporarily swap your profile picture for a photo of your loved one, which will serve as a visual cue there's something different going on that deserves attention.

And finally, while there are numerous websites to help memorialize loved ones (www.forevermissed.com and www.legacy.com are two examples), I am drawn to the platform Zaslow and her sisters chose to honor their dad: a website through WordPress. Unlike many purpose-built online services, WordPress doesn't charge a monthly fee and has search-engine visibility. Their website, www.rememberingzazz.com, is how I came across Zaslow's eulogy for her father, which they posted in its entirety.

> Since the accident, I haven't let go of one of your button down shirts. It smells just like you when you used to come home from work or a speech. It was the smell of comfort. It was the best smell in the entire world. It meant you were home safe and sound and you were ours.

28.

Generate a Digital
Wave of Light

Worldwide Candle Lighting is an immense annual event run by The
Compassionate Friends, a nonprofit based outside Chicago. Similar to
how New Year's Eve unfolds, the event kicks off at the same time no
matter where you live on the planet—the second Sunday in December
at 7:00 PM—when individuals light candles at home or in large groups

in memory of children who have died. The goal is to bridge countries and time zones by creating a wave of light that lasts twenty-four hours.

This Forget Me Not guides you in building on the Worldwide Candle Lighting concept, customizing it to create an opportunity for remembering at any time of year. Here's what you do:

- Create a hashtag on Twitter. For example, if your loved one's name were Lynn, your hashtag could be #rememberinglynn.
- Pick a time for your remembrance—a birthday, holiday, or special occasion—and let your inner circle know.
- When the date arrives, encourage everyone to light a candle, take a picture of it, and post it to Twitter using the hashtag.

Jennifer Jett, a mom of two in Raleigh, North Carolina, introduced me to Worldwide Candle Lighting. Her connection with the ritual derives from having lost her son, Grayson, in a car accident when he was fourteen months old. Jett now looks forward to Worldwide Candle Lighting every year. "I have people lighting candles from California to Germany. It's amazing," she wrote me. "I also love it because it's an activity I can share with my older son Jackson. He was five years old when his brother died, and it's something positive we can do together. We both want to keep Grayson's memory alive and this is one way we can do that side by side."

To learn more, visit www.compassionatefriends.org/News_Events/Special-Events/Worldwide_Candle_Lighting.aspx.

29.

Leave a Random
Note of Kindness

The Kindness Project invites you to commit a random act of kindness in memory of a loved one. The initiative, the brainchild of MISS Foundation, a national organization supporting families who have lost children, is available free to anyone who has experienced loss of any kind.

To participate, download a preprinted Kindness Project card from the organization's website. Each note has "THIS RANDOM ACT OF KINDNESS" written across the top and "DONE IN LOVING MEMORY OF" stamped along the bottom, followed by a blank space for the name of your loved one. Projects have included baking cookies for a police station and adding coins to a stranger's parking meter. The organization's website (www.missfoundation.org) has a helpful "Get Ideas" page.

30.

Crowdsource
Family History

My mother organized over-the-top family reunions. She'd get T-shirts
in various solid colors—red, green, canary yellow, and blue—and give
them out when everyone arrived. Color assignments weren't random;
each represented a branch of our family tree, and wearing them was a
source of excitement and conversation. She brought similar enthusiasm

to her off-season role as family historian—updating the family tree throughout the year with birth and marriage information, and gathering photos to include alongside many relatives' names. I remember thinking how much easier it would be if all that work was a communal activity, shared equally by her sister and cousins. But that was before the digital era, when splitting the workload would have been difficult.

It's with this realization that I encourage you to devote a picnic table at your next family reunion to preserving and sharing photos. Before the big day, ask relatives to gather albums and any loose pictures they have. Pictures of unidentified ancestors are particularly great to bring along. Using Shoebox, a free app from www.ancestry.com, family members can snap each other's photos and get help identifying people and places they don't recognize. And while smartphone cameras can digitize dozens of photos in seconds, Shoebox is useful because it has auto-flattening technology that digitally corrects tattered and bent edges. Another benefit is the ability to upload images directly to your ancestry.com family tree.

I believe my mom would have relished this kind of collective memory-keeping—especially the chance to share pictures, swap stories, and work collaboratively. She also would have appreciated the pizzazz a bit of tech adds to a reunion, too.

31.

Digitize Family Recipes and Make Them an Indelible Part of Your Life

After Jonathan Safran Foer published his two wildly successful novels *Everything is Illuminated* and *Extremely Loud and Incredibly Close* (both of which were adapted into movies), he published *Eating Animals*, a far-reaching investigation into what we eat and how our habits related to food are formed.

Foer concludes early in the book that our relationship with food is important to understand because it represents so much more than sustenance. His grandmother's chicken with carrots wasn't delicious simply because she prepared it a certain way; it was delicious because of both what the dish represented (continuity between generations) and what it prompted (conversation over the dinner table). He writes: "I came to learn that food serves two parallel purposes: it nourishes and it helps you remember. Eating and storytelling are inseparable."

How, then, can we hold on to these specific tastes and the stories they help us tell? The answer lies in preserving recipes in perpetuity so dishes can be replicated again and again. Here are two ideas for doing just that.

Using Google Docs (www.google.com/docs/about) you could create a family recipe archive available to anyone who opens the document. To do this you'd invite relatives to contribute their favorite dishes and desserts, uploaded on recipe cards so everyone can take pleasure in a loved one's familiar handwriting. The project could stop right there. Or, for more ambitious types, consider designing a professional-quality cookbook, which relatives could order with the click of a mouse. These cookbooks could be further enhanced with family photographs.

You could also memorialize a beloved recipe as the focal point of a custom-made plate or platter. Beth Digman runs Prairie Hills Pottery from her home studio in Dodgeville, Wisconsin. She takes a JPEG of the recipe and transfers it onto a fine, food-safe ceramic piece from her shop—which may be rectangular, oval, or square, with smooth or scalloped edges. The entire process, including glazing and firing in her kiln, takes approximately fifty hours. I can attest that the recipe transfer is permanent and that the finished product is beautiful.

For more, visit www.prairiehillspottery.com.

32.

Transform
Their Handwriting

Allison Hansen's mother used to scribble notes and put them in her lunchbox every day. "Sometimes she would write a poem, sometimes just a simple message telling me to smile and have a good day," she told me, fondly recalling the loving ritual. "I still have most of them and keep them in a box with other cards and letters she wrote me over the

years." So when, four years after her mother had passed away, Hansen was planning her wedding in 2014, she could think of no better way to honor her memory than by incorporating a fragment of her mother's handwriting into the special day.

From one of her mother's lunchbox notes, Hansen scanned the words "*Love, Mom.*" Once she uploaded the file to a jewelry company in California, the signature was engraved onto a charm, which Hansen could wear as a necklace or wrap around her bouquet. She reflected, "It was such a simple yet powerful reminder of her unconditional love and support."

Signatures can be engraved into virtually any metal and used to decorate rings, keychains, even a pair of cufflinks. Hansen worked with Los Angeles–based Emily Jane Designs (www.emilyjanejewelry.com), but you can likely find a jeweler near you who does similar work. If that's not an option, I have found many wonderful artists by searching "handwritten jewelry" and "handwriting jewelry" on www.etsy.com.

Jewelers can also capture handprints, footprints, even doodles. Kylie Newton wears a silver ring designed with the thumbprint of her brother, who died of cancer when he was just a few weeks shy of his sixteenth birthday. The ring was crafted by Brent & Jess (www.brentjess.com), a jewelry company in Maine, using a thumbprint her mother had found on a project he'd done in elementary school.

"He was the only boy," Newton, who was twelve when he died, told me. "He was also the oldest, and I cherish every memory with him. The ring lets me see a physical part of my brother every day, even when I'm doing the dishes."

Newton's mom commissioned a similar ring. For her, the best part of wearing it is feeling her son's fingerprint every time she rubs it. "It brings him right back to me," she said. "It helps me acknowledge my son and his life."

33.

Be Creative
with Video

I thank my daughter for sparking the following ideas. One afternoon, Lexi bounded home from a play date eager to show me her latest creation. She and her best friend had spent the afternoon making a Flipagram out of dozens of selfies.

The Flipagram app uses photos on your smartphone to create fun and quirky videos. You control the amount of time each picture is displayed, the shortest length being just .01 seconds. The result is a fast-paced movie that animates even the most ordinary images. You can also add music and share the videos via Instagram, Facebook, and YouTube.

It didn't take me long to see an unexpected and thrilling opportunity with this. By making a Flipagram, I could take a few pictures out of their current, underappreciated context of photo albums and present them in the more inviting, contemporary framework of social media. All that was required was downloading the Flipagram app and selecting a few pictures from my phone. While Lexi helped me make the video, I shared with her stories about her grandparents and other relatives she never got to know.

Flipagrams got me thinking about other opportunities for making photos and home videos more enjoyable and memorable. The following ideas are the ones I'm most enthusiastic about, some inspired by my career in television news:

- To intensify the viewing experience, don't play home movies raw. Instead, edit them to make them shorter and more digestible.

- Lay down a soundtrack. Since music helps create mood, use a vocal or instrumental piece you find particularly evocative.

- Add captions to identify people, places, and important dates. This makes watching more entertaining and underscores critical information. It also ensures details aren't lost for future generations.

- And finally, when your new social-media friendly videos are ready, launch a YouTube channel. Watching home movies is great; sharing them with friends and family amplifies the experience.

34.

Send a
Meeting Maker

For many years, on the anniversaries of my parents' deaths I waited impatiently for the phone to ring, hoping friends and family would reach out to me as they once had. But even those closest to me would often forget. They weren't being heartless—they were just busy and distracted. And I understood.

Gradually, I've come to recognize that anniversaries are frequently difficult because so often we remember alone. To counter this, I realized I could send a calendar invitation to a small group of people reminding them of my parents' anniversaries. That way, I reasoned, I'd be assured a supportive text or phone call on the two days I needed them most.

Here's how I did it on my iPhone: I went to CALENDAR, pressed the plus (+) symbol to ADD EVENT, plugged in the appropriate TITLE and DATE, set the invitation to repeat EVERY YEAR, and then chose a few email addresses from my CONTACTS list to whom I wanted the invitation sent. I did this process twice—for the anniversary of each parent's death.

I must say, I got really excited about this innovation—and I'm not the only one. When I mentioned the idea to a friend who'd lost her sister twelve years earlier, she immediately set about making her own calendar invitation. It wouldn't be stretching the truth to describe her reaction as giddy. *Seeing the opportunity* and *seizing it* can make you very happy.

35.

Embrace
Throwback Thursday

Throwback Thursday is another way to integrate your loved one into your life online. Throwback Thursday is a social media trend that encourages users to share favorite memories on a weekly basis. While commonly used to post childhood photos, it also provides the perfect opportunity to post pictures of loved ones. It can be remarkably satisfying to see their image pop up in your Facebook or Twitter feed, especially if he or she died before the digital era.

It certainly was gratifying for me. Since my mother died in 1996, for years after, looking at photos was an entirely private experience. I could only talk about them or share them with someone who was physically with me—looking at the pictures on my walls or sitting on my couch flipping through an album. But on Thursday, January 22, 2015, all that changed: I finally embraced #TBT as a tool for remembering my parents. The picture I uploaded was taken in 1970. My mother and father are walking barefoot on a beach, smiling broadly. My dad has a snorkel mask strapped around his forehead and my mom, pregnant with me, is carrying a pair of flippers. At the bottom of the photo, my mother wrote in now-faded blue ink, "5 WKS TO GO."

Finding this picture and sharing it as part of Throwback Thursday put me in a great frame of mind. And while it may sound overboard to you, to me it was like they were temporarily resurrected. My mother and father were a tangible part of my life that day (eliciting present-day comments and feedback!), and I relished how it made me feel—joyous, full, nearly complete. And each time I choose to post pictures of my parents on a Thursday, I feel afresh that fabulous and positive surge of connection.

36.

Hang On to Meaningful Posts and Emails

Host of CNN's Reliable Sources, Brian Stelter, often pulls up emails to remind him of his dear friend David Carr, late columnist for *The New York Times*. Since Stelter's father had died of heart disease when he was fifteen, Carr became a father figure to him, and thought of Stelter like a son. When Carr, collapsing in the paper's newsroom, suddenly died in

February 2015, Stelter wrote a moving tribute to their relationship for the website *Modern Loss*. The piece was an ode, really, to their mundane and genuinely affectionate emails.

"When I reread his emails," Stelter began, "I can hear him uttering each word. Sometimes they're signed 'M'wah.' Sometimes they're blank, with only a subject line: 'What's the haps?' . . ."

The emails that are serious or poignant, like the one that arrived in Stelter's in-box a few days before he got married, carry a different weight. In that message, Carr lovingly wrote: "'Get a little jewel to send over b4 she walks up aisle. Send over With flower girl. That way she always has a lasting totem of that day.'" Stelter both followed Carr's advice and archived that email.

Every email from his friend, stretching over nearly a decade, is a message Stelter can't foresee deleting. Carr's history is "always just a few keystrokes away," Stelter explains, and his emails "help me remember."

Emails and posts don't have to live only on your computer. Print a few for your bulletin board, or even get one or more properly framed. While normally ephemeral, your loved one's digital footprint can serve as a powerful and tangible reminder of your relationship.

37.

Find Official
Documents

Digging into family history has never been easier to do. These days, thanks to the National Digital Newspaper Program—a partnership between the Library of Congress and the National Endowment for the Humanities—it's possible to search more than eight million pages of newspaper without ever leaving home. And if you take into account www.newspaperarchive.com, which calls itself the "world's largest news-paper archive," claiming nearly two billion articles online, you might never have to get off the couch to find what you're looking for. But after the search is complete, what else can you do with all those birth notices, wedding announcements, and headlines you printed?

I encourage you to remove your amassed collection from your filing cabinet and infuse all those documents with greater meaning. Forget Me Not #2 (A Different Kind of Scrapbook) is a great place to begin. For one thing, by cutting up your search results and pasting them into your scrapbook you give yourself the opportunity to put all that family research and history into context. Likewise, historical records can be used to decoupage a Memory-Keeper (Forget Me Not #15)—or, if you're willing to go bigger, a piece of unfinished wooden furniture. End tables, stools, and nightstands are all worthwhile options that would enable you to regularly commune with the fruits of your labor. I also suggest printing out period advertisements. These images create wonderful texture and interest to decoupage projects and Biographical Scrapbooks.

The National Digital Newspaper Program makes its archives available through its Chronicling America website, www.chroniclingamerica.loc.gov. As of this printing, American newspapers are searchable from the years 1836–1922. For information published as far back as 1690, you can use the U.S. Newspaper Directory.

38.

Hire a Personal
Historian

There's no doubt that preserving family history requires patience and time. If you're short on both but have the means and interest, I recommend working with a professional.

Personal historians do all the heavy lifting for you: wading through photographs and documents and researching factual loose ends. They also craft your family's story so it's intelligible and captivating, helping you to create a book, make a video, or build a family website from the material they've catalogued or helped you collect.

The Association of Personal Historians offers a directory of its members and the services they offer on its website: www.personalhistorians.org.

39.

Fabricate
History

Stephanie Rich never met her grandfather. But nearly eighty years after he spent a summer traipsing through Europe in 1931, she set out to replicate his journey. For three months during the summer of 2009, Rich, traveling solo and armed with photocopies of snapshots her grandfather took on vacation, embarked on a "lifelong dream of retracing his steps and taking matching photographs at the exact locations he had visited," she wrote in her kindhearted travelogue, *A Followed Path: Travels with My Grandfather*.

The trip wouldn't be easy; Leo Rich had visited England, France, Germany, the Netherlands, Austria, and Italy. Nor would be her goal of replicating all his photos; while he documented nearly 180 of his pictures, many were of places that would be hard to pinpoint—a random canal in Venice, or an uncited photo taken of the vast Dolomites. But in the end, Rich managed to find most of the same bridges and overlooks where her grandfather had once stood. She also walked the same streets, meandered through the same piazzas, and sat in the same churches, museums, and gardens. In every location she replicated, as closely as she could, the photo her grandfather had taken seventy-eight years earlier.

Rich recalls her trip as a successful mission. With her grandfather serving as tour director, Rich allowed "an incredibly important figure in my life to guide me as if he were still alive today, as if he knew me and knew what I would enjoy, what would open my eyes and what would have a profound impact on me." The experience, she reflected, "was the closest I've ever felt to someone watching over me."

A Followed Path is a fantastic example of how technology can be used to build connections between generations. And the book's juxtaposition of her grandfather's black and white photographs with Rich's color, high-resolution shots is deeply moving. While Leo Rich introduced Stephanie to the Palace of Fontainebleau and Lake Como, with today's technology, it is as if Stephanie were able to introduce her grandfather to twenty-first-century Europe as well.

For the technologically inclined, there's also the possibility of bridging generations by using the software program Adobe Photoshop. To help the younger set see for themselves the physical traits they've inherited from family members, start with a good facial-depicting photo from contrasting generations, one younger and one elder. Then edit the images together so it appears they were taken at the same time. With the resulting product, the newest generation will be able to observe something extraordinary—they actually *do* have "Grandma's smile" and "Uncle Willie's" eyes!

This project is also remarkably fun for adults. I asked Rich if she ever thought about Photoshopping an image together of her and Grandpa Leo. Her enthusiastic response suggested that project might be next.

40.

Record a Digital
Walking Tour

This Forget Me Not is a great idea if you're planning a vacation to your ancestral hometown: record a digital audio walking tour, similar to the guided commentary available at museums. (This item is, admittedly, best suited to the tech-savvy.) First, research the most important points you'd like your family to see and plot the best route. Then, pulling information

from relatives and online sources, create an audio recording in which you describe the significance of each landmark. Armed with your finished digital file, family members can benefit from the commentary as they traverse the itinerary step by step. And those among them most comfortable with technology can perhaps record their own observations, building an audio scrapbook.

41.

Craft Their
Image Into Art

Dutch artist Miranda van Dijk creates the most astonishing memory art I've ever seen. Working with photos sent to her, she transfers the image onto a piece of unbleached cotton, coats it with starch, and painstakingly crafts the stiffened fabric into the shape of a flower, leaf, or set of branches. I love the idea of using her designs as meaningful centerpieces, decorative chair backs, or nestling them into a wedding bouquet or canopy. Van Dijk's work was inspired by the loss of her grandmother, and it shows—she tenderly incorporates her personal experience and sensitivity into each piece she makes.

Visit her site at www.puuranders.nl.

42.

Make a
Game of It

Given how much we can do with technology these days, it would be a shame to not harness its benefits for children. Personalize a deck of cards with photographs of living family members and those you've lost. By integrating *all* your loved ones, children are seamlessly taught to value every relationship in their lives. The same sense of recognition can come from customizing a board book for a toddler or designing your own memory game. And, if you work with the eco-friendly website www.paperculture.com to create one of these projects or others, the company will plant a tree in recognition of every purchase—giving customers the opportunity to dedicate that tree to whomever they wish.

3 *Not Just Holidays*

The urge to remember can happen anytime, anywhere. When a song pops on the radio. While eating a certain food. When crossing the street. We are generally well equipped to negotiate this terrain around the holidays—family and friends expect a certain amount of wistfulness and nostalgia. But it's equally important, if not more so, to have tools for remembering during those off-times, those under-the-radar moments when memories catch you by surprise or when you simply crave a chance to reflect.

The Forget Me Nots in this section invite you to take advantage of all your senses: you'll find approaches here for using your sight, hearing, taste, touch, and smell. There are concepts related to music and cooking, talking and journaling, and favorite words and sayings. The ideas will also encourage you to transform routine and ordinary experiences—like getting together with friends—into memory-preserving opportunities.

There is no reason why remembering should be limited to a particular season or date on the calendar. Packing away your feelings until the "right" time of year honors neither your feelings nor your relationship. Celebrating your loved one can happen any time of year, whenever you feel the tug, *for as long as it makes you happy.*

43.

Host a Memory Bash

Invite friends over for a lively evening of eating, drinking, and keeping the memory of loved ones alive with quick-and-easy projects that encourage conversation. In between cocktails and hors d'oeuvres, guests can create no-mess, grown-up versions of Make a Frame (Forget Me Not #18) or Create a Memory Magnet (Forget Me Not #19).

To do this, you'll need frames, a few pairs of scissors, and sheets of epoxy stickers and magnetic backing. Set up tables and chairs with ample working space for your guests, who should each bring two cherished photos. As the party unfolds, in addition to hanging out and drinking wine, friends can trim their photos to the size of their new frames and Memory Magnets. Finished products drive discussion and should be kept on display throughout the night.

The best frames for a Memory Bash are different from Make a Frames. In that version, kids are involved, and part of the fun is getting messy. Here, either all the decorating is done when guests go home (when there's sufficient time to let frames dry) or no painting, staining, or gluing is required at all. If your friends aren't crafty, just buy a few cute frames before the party and let each guest pick their favorite one.

44.

Start a
Remembrance Chain

The benefit of this Forget Me Not is that it builds connection and anticipation at times when everyone involved may need a little more of both—either immediately following a death or years later when an added dose of reflection can feel especially good.

To begin, buy a journal. Next, establish a list of eager participants, and print or write out separate mailing labels for each. Then, mail the journal to the first person on the list; be sure to include with the package all the remaining mailing labels. Each participant should record in the journal a special memory—be it funny story or serious anecdote—and sign the remembrance, and then forward it and the mailing labels to the next contact on the list.

I recommend having the individual who was closest to the loved one be the last person to receive the Remembrance Chain, which by then has become a deeply meaningful gift he or she will always treasure.

45.

Build
a Refuge

After my father died, my stepmother, Cheryl, craved a quiet place outdoors to think about my dad—ideally in a setting readily accessible in
all types of weather.

Cheryl's perfect spot was right in the backyard they had shared. Off
to the side there's a small patch of land hidden from the neighbors' view.

She cleared out a few weeds, bought an iron bench at a garage sale, and that was about it. A refuge was born.

My favorite part of Cheryl's retreat, however, is the path she made to get there. She gathered a large number of medium-sized stones and carefully positioned them one after the other until a line of rocks stretched from the side of the house to the bench. And then, over the course of several visits, she asked my children and my brother's children to help her paint each stone with a different stanza from *We Remember Them*, a poem by Rabbis Sylvan Kamens and Jack Riemer. Here's how the poem begins, adapted below:

> *At the rising of the sun and at its going down*
> *We remember them.*
> *At the blowing of the wind and in the chill of winter*
> *We remember them.*
> *At the opening of the buds and in the rebirth of spring*
> *We remember them.*
> *At the shining of the sun and in the warmth of summer*
> *We remember them.*
> *At the rustling of the leaves and in the beauty of autumn*
> *We remember them.*

At the beginning of the year and at its end
We remember them.

As long as we live, they too will live;
for they are now a part of us,
as we remember them.

For my kids, helping their grandmother build this private space created an unexpected opening to talk about their grandfather. My daughter never met my father, and my son was only eighteen months old when he died, so the hours spent painting words on rocks became time spent hearing stories about my dad. I will forever be grateful to Cheryl for orchestrating such an opportunity.

Building an outdoor refuge doesn't require a lot of effort or space. You can use a chair instead of a bench or simply spread a blanket on the ground. There's no obligation to mark a trail. The goal is simply giving yourself the time and a location to be alone with your thoughts. And for that reason, it's essential to recognize that a sanctuary doesn't have to be outdoors—you can assign refuge status to any spot you dedicate for reflection, even your sofa—as long as it offers you a quiet place to remember.

46.

Grow
Daffodils

One of the most uplifting gifts I've ever heard of giving someone in a time of loss is a wicker basket full of daffodil bulbs. The idea is for the recipient to plant, if possible, one bulb for every year the loved one lived. Daffodils are the perfect flower for such a happiness-inducing project: as perennials, they'll come back spring after spring—and they're virtually indestructible.

Becky Heath, along with her husband Brent, run Brent and Becky's, a twenty-eight-acre daffodil farm and distribution center in Gloucester,

Virginia, that's been family-owned since 1900. "Daffodils are some of the world's more resilient flowers," Becky Heath told me. "They're pest proof, rodent proof, and deer proof. Your idea is great because it would be very hard not to do it successfully."

What advice does Heath have for growing daffodils? In addition to choosing a sunny spot, here are a few tips to keep in mind:

- Daffodils are best planted in the fall, after the first frost, because the bulbs prefer cool soil. If you live in a southern climate, stick with planting jonquils or tazettas, as these daffodils are better suited for warmer temperatures.
- Pay attention during the summer (when the bulbs are "sleeping") to how wet your soil is; like people, Heath joked, daffodil bulbs "prefer a dry bed, not a wet one."
- Plant each bulb at a depth of three times their height, spacing them three times their width apart.

You can buy daffodil bulbs online or at your local gardening center. The benefit of ordering them through Brent and Becky's (www.brentandbeckys-bulbs.com) or a similar shop is that you don't have to wait until September or October to make your purchase. You can order anytime; your shipment will be sent only when the bulbs are ready to be planted.

47.

Choose the Right Words
and Say Them Again and Again

Dr. Kathy Hirsh-Pasek, codirector of the Temple Infant & Child Laboratory at Temple University, convinced me several years ago that *how* we talk about loved ones plays a critical role in the way *others* remember them.

I interviewed Hirsh-Pasek for *Parentless Parents*. I asked her then if she thought it mattered if mothers and fathers, when talking to their children, refer to their own parents as "Mom" and "Dad" or "Grandma" and "Grandpa." She told me:

> How we frame language is important, especially at the youngest ages. Children are egocentric by nature and want to understand how things relate to them. Anytime we can make what we say more concrete and more connected to who they are, children will find it more meaningful.

What does that mean in practice? If you're telling your daughter a story about your brother, say "your uncle," not "my brother."

While writing this book I reached out again to Hirsh-Pasek. This time I wanted to know if it's possible to predict how well a loved one will be remembered based on how often their name is brought up in conversation. Her reply: "Memories are reinforced by conversation. We remember more if we talk about our memories more. Mentioning a loved one out of context will never be as effective as talking about them as part of a story—a silly anecdote or lesson you're trying to teach. Good stories live on."

In this regard, especially for readers who have young children, Hirsh-Pasek says incorporating a loved one into a bedtime story can be helpful. That's because bedtime stories are entertaining and involve repeating names over and over again. Likewise, I urge you to pay special attention to the next Forget Me Not, #48, and remember the words "grilled cheese and spaghetti."

The best advice, though, is simply giving yourself permission to say your loved one's name out loud. According to Hirsh-Pasek, "Repetition is the number one way to ensure a name isn't forgotten."

48.

Cook Grilled Cheese
and Spaghetti

Gwyneth Paltrow spends a lot of time cooking with her children. "Fire and knives, no wonder my son is obsessed with it all," the Oscar-winning actress writes in her cookbook *My Father's Daughter: Delicious, Easy Recipes Celebrating Family & Togetherness*. But for Paltrow, food prep is a lot more than busy work to keep her son and daughter entertained.

"I always feel closest to my father, who was the love of my life until his death in 2002, when I am in the kitchen," she explains.

The recipes in Paltrow's book are mostly for everyday foods—salads, burgers, sandwiches, oatmeal, and muffins—and each is accompanied by a personal anecdote. We learn intimate details about her family with recipes for her dad's "world-famous pancakes"; a signature crab entrée reminds Paltrow of a grandmother who was "amazing at a party." Paltrow's book is a fantastic reminder that the familiar meals and desserts we already prepare—the ones we likely make by heart and which rouse our warmest memories—present perfect occasions for talking about our loved ones.

Foods that prompt conversation don't have to be fancy—they can be as simple as grilled cheese and spaghetti. Of course, by "grilled cheese and spaghetti" I mean any dish you associate with your loved one. The point is merely to lower the bar and embrace even the smallest tidbits of opportunity.

Repeat this mantra—"Grilled Cheese and Spaghetti." It'll remind you when you're cooking or sharing a meal to pass along the stories that are probably already on your mind.

49.

Work with
a Medium

One weekend recently I did something I thought I'd never do—I attempted to connect with my loved ones through a medium. But my interest, which was piqued five years earlier when I read Lisa Miller's *Heaven: Our Enduring Fascination With the Afterlife*, skyrocketed when I pored through Claire Bidwell Smith's *After This: When Life*

Is Over, Where Do We Go? Miller's experience with a medium left her "doubtful"; Smith's multiyear exploration prompted her to proclaim, "The beliefs I once held about this life being all there is seem naïve and unnecessarily restrictive."

When I finished Smith's book it was nineteen years after my mother's death and fourteen years since my father's. By then, I was finally open to giving the whole thing a try.

It would be hard to find more mediums in one place than in Lily Dale, New York, so that's where I headed. Lily Dale Assembly (lilydaleassembly. com) is a gated community about fifty-three miles south of Buffalo, and the bulk of its visitors, more than 30,000 reported annually, come during the "season"—from the end of June through early September. People are invited to walk door to door or make appointments to work with any of the village's fifty or so registered mediums. Each sets his or her own schedule and fees, and most mediums have clipboards with sign-up sheets right outside their homes.

To protect my identity, I didn't schedule meetings before I arrived. My books *Always Too Soon* and *Parentless Parents* contain a treasure-trove of information about my life and losses. I've also written dozens of articles for CNN.com, The Huffington Post, and The Daily Beast—all of which can be found online. I chose two mediums (a man and a woman) with whom I signed up on the spot, providing only my first name.

The sessions brought me to tears. One of the mediums knew I had been closer to my mother than my father; the other correctly intuited that my parents had died young and from cancer. My father wanted me to know he was sorry he and my mom couldn't make their marriage work. How could the medium have known they'd gotten a divorce? Both parents said they were proud of what I'd achieved, pleased I've taught my children they are unconditionally loved, and love me and are always with me. And while both mediums got plenty of facts wrong, they presented so many that were right it was hard for me to dismiss everything summarily. Was I being taken for a ride or were these encounters, even portions of them, real? Did it even matter?

The only takeaway I know for sure is *the sessions made me happy.* Yes, I was emotional, but spending the entire weekend focusing on nothing else but my parents was an unexpected gift. Just as yoga enthusiasts go on retreats to heighten their practice, I was able to both commune with my losses for forty-eight hours and meet other people drawn to do the same. I hadn't felt so connected to my mom and dad (or a group of strangers, for that matter) in a long time, and it felt freeing and blissful, a true and powerful release.

Lily Dale is an odd, endearing community. It is also a full-on keeping-the-memory-of-your-loved-one-alive vacation destination. There are restaurants, hotels, a lake for boating and swimming, and stores to buy crystals, books, and souvenirs. There's a DAILY EVENTS board listing optional activities. When I visited, I went to an 8:30 AM meditation at the Healing Temple and a 5:30 PM gathering at Inspiration Stump—during which, like a frenzied game of speed dating, multiple mediums offered messages to dozens of visitors for nearly one hour. I also joined approximately eight hundred people to hear one of the most popular mediums in the world, the effervescent and charming James Van Praagh.

Cassadaga Spiritualist Camp, located about thirty-five miles north of Orlando, Florida, is another option to consider. While the spot itself is smaller than Lily Dale and has fewer mediums on-site, the offerings are similar. It's also possible to work with mediums by phone. Both communities list phone numbers and email addresses for their "certified" and "registered" mediums on their websites.

For more, go to www.cassadaga.org.

Despite remaining skeptical, I agree with Claire Bidwell Smith that there's something "very worthwhile" in these sessions when they go well. She states that even if it's simulated or imagined, "finding ways, no matter how far-fetched, to feel connected to that person is the very thing that can enable us to move forward."

50.

Write it Down

We always think we'll remember our loved ones' funny or poignant sayings. This idea (and the one that follows in Forget Me Not #51) ensures you'll never forget.

Buy a small notebook. Choose one small enough to go anywhere you go—via the glove compartment of your car, your purse, or the back pocket of your jeans. Commit phrases to paper as soon as they come to you. Refer to them later.

The power of this project is not derived from how much money you spend on the notebook; the impact comes from the words and phrases you choose to preserve.

51.

Stencil a Favorite Saying

The day her nationally syndicated talk show debuted, Meredith Vieira gave Matt Lauer a live, behind-the-scenes tour of her set for the TODAY show. Just before entering, Vieira told Lauer, "You are about to see my home away from home."

Artwork by Vieira's three children lines the studio walls. Family photos are everywhere—and not just the ones visible on camera. When I visited her, I noticed snapshots in the holding area for members of the studio audience, including a picture of Vieira and her father when she graduated college. But my favorite inclusion is the blue rectangular sign hanging prominently over the stage's faux fireplace. Reading, in white lettering, DR. EDWIN VIEIRA, the sign had once adorned Vieira's father's office—and Vieira celebrated his memory by positioning this keepsake in the middle of her set.

Even without inheriting such a meaningful item, we can borrow from Vieira's aesthetic, making particular words and phrases an indelible part of our home as well. One way to do this is to stencil a short word or saying directly on a wall. Craft warehouses such as Michaels, Jo-Ann, and A.C. Moore sell stencils in various sizes, some several feet tall.

If you prefer a less conspicuous project, you can simply paint a small sign. Little signs can be leaned against a bathroom mirror or displayed on a bookshelf.

For both big and small signs, I recommend using a plain font so the words are easy to read.

52.

Get
Inked

In 2007, singer Kanye West's mother passed away. Nearly eight years later, West got a tattoo of his mother's birthday inked in Roman numerals on one of his wrists. "I talked him out of getting a face tattoo . . . for now," his wife, Kim Kardashian, posted on Instagram.

Humankind's earliest tattoos, which have been traced back 5,300 years, were likely used for healing. "Iceman," a mummy discovered along the Italian-Austrian border in 1991, has a pattern of linear marks covering nearly every joint in his body. 61 have been detected so far, two in the shape of a cross—one on the right knee, the other on the left ankle close to the Achilles tendon. Professor Walter Leitner, an archaeologist at University of Innsbruck in Austria and one of a small group of scientists with access to Iceman, says the placement of the markings strongly indicates an expected medicinal benefit. "X-rays found pathological signs of overstraining exactly in these regions," he wrote me in an email. "The man must have suffered violent pains."

While tattoo-therapy is still used in some parts of the world, it's not surprising the driving force behind getting tattoos would change over time from a perceived physical need to an emotional one. Today, legendary tattoo artist Lyle Tuttle—who's inscribed thousands of people since 1949, including Cher, Janis Joplin, and every member of the Allman Brothers Band—says tattoos are often used to connect people to the deceased. Tattoos are "external decorations for internal feelings.

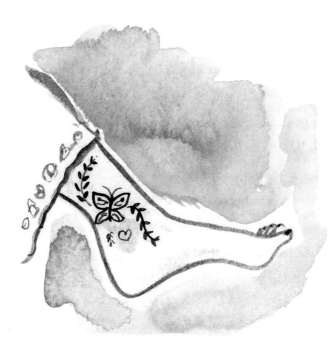

What better way to show your emotion or dedication to someone than to have a symbol of that connection indelibly etched into your skin."

Tattoos also offer a private reservoir of strength. A few months after her sister died of cancer, Alicia Barry got a large flower tattooed on her left shoulder blade. The yellow petals and green stem are visible to anyone who sees her in a tank top, but no one would ever know the backstory unless they asked. "Sunflowers were my sister's favorite flower," Barry told me. "I got it on my left side because we're both lefties. It also helps me remember she was real. It's proof of her existence."

Is there a symbol that fills you with good memories? Perhaps it's a shooting star, a butterfly, or simply your loved one's initials. Maybe, like Kanye West, there's a date of significance to you. Tattoos of every kind can keep your loved one's memory alive. Every drawing tells a story—whether for the world or just for yourself.

53.

Retrace
Your Steps

The song "These Foolish Things" recounts a long list of sights, sounds, objects, and places that conjure up memories of a lost love. Take a cue from that popular standard to kindle your own recollections. Go back to that restaurant. Return to the hotel. Feel gratitude that what you had is worth missing—and can remain with you.

54.

Keep
Doing It

This Forget Me Not builds on the last. For this one, consider all the activities you and your loved one did together. If you enjoyed ice skating, go to the rink. If hiking was more your speed, climb that next peak.

When we mourn our loved ones we also tend to grieve the hobbies we shared. You don't have to suffer this double loss.

55.

Perpetuate
Their Passions

Volunteer your time to organizations that support the values or interests of those you've lost. What cause or activity brought meaning to their lives? There are a number of ways you could go about extending their impact. For example, if your best friend cared about animal rescue, you could socialize cats or walk dogs at the local animal shelter. Or you could foster a litter of kittens. You might also take your dog to visit a nursing home. (It so happens that nurturing animals is a great way to process grief, so this route has multiple benefits.)

Regardless of the initiative you undertake, open yourself to feeling your loved one with you, rooting you on.

56.

Listen
to Music

Make playlists of your loved one's favorite songs, especially of music you enjoyed together.

57.

Expand
Your Circle

One excellent way to keep the memory of loved ones alive is to talk about them with people who knew them—whether *you* know those individuals or not. Chat with former coworkers and neighbors. Learn more from their teachers or club leaders. You could even heighten the experience by planning a full-fledged Connection Vacation (Forget Me Not #72).

58.

Give
Objects Away

There are likely many people who knew and cared about your loved one, but not everyone will have a tangible memento. Maybe you have too many. Items that no longer give you pleasure may make somebody else incredibly happy.

59.

Donate
to a Museum

Trinkets of every stripe might be of interest to historical societies. The National September 11 Memorial & Museum still receives donations of shoes, clothing, ID cards, even telephone messages. Such objects, now in the care of professional preservationists and curators, ensure the men and women who once owned them will never be forgotten. Consider what types of objects you have. Object-centric museums maintain vast collections of items, be they ceramics or costumes, sports memorabilia or stamps, textiles, or typewriters.

60.

Establish a
New Spring Ritual

Many stories exist for how the flower forget-me-not got its name. One version can be traced back to the early nineteenth century, when a man apparently drowned trying to pick the charming blue flower for his fiancée. Another claims the bloom used to be given as a token of a lover's faithfulness. No matter the account, the heart of the story remains the same: imploring those who are deeply connected to never forget their bonds. As such, it's only appropriate to integrate these little flowers into your spring routine.

Every year I look forward to the satisfying ritual of buying a small pot of forget-me-nots—which come in pink and white as well as the familiar blue—to place somewhere I'll see all day. For the few weeks the flowers last, I enjoy the living, physical reminder of the relationships I had with those I've lost.

Melanie Pyle, director of interior displays at Smithsonian Gardens at the Smithsonian Institution, says forget-me-nots will last longest indoors if they're kept out of direct sunlight. She also emphasized that, though forget-me-nots like to be consistently moist, they are especially vulnerable to overwatering, so tend to your loving reminder with care.

61.

Call Attention
to Their Absence

Embrace milestones like weddings and christenings as opportunities to reflect. Light a candle in their honor. List their name on a program. Leave an empty chair at your gathering. I especially like the idea of recognizing the event's significance by writing a letter—to yourself or to someone else—detailing what the occasion would have meant to your loved one.

62.

Celebrate the
Hardest Days

On their birthday, eat their favorite ice cream. On the anniversary of their death, enjoy their favorite meal.

63.

Foster
Serendipity

Grab a photo album and leave it in a high-traffic area—on the kitchen counter, for example, or the dining room table. Do something nearby while you wait expectantly for a family member to walk by and flip through the pages. As if by coincidence, be available to answer any questions or share a story. There's no need to display the album permanently; success comes from it being an atypical sighting.

64.

Give Memories
100 Percent

Linger over pictures. Read old letters and birthday cards. Watch home movies.

Devote an entire day to remembering.

4 *Monthly Guide*

While this book presents ideas for remembering at any time of year, calendar-specific dates are especially helpful for framing additional opportunities. Every season offers a fresh chance to honor loved ones, each deserves special recognition and treatment.

The Forget Me Nots in this section are presented in chronological order, beginning with New Year's and ending with Christmas. Holidays that can't be pinned to an exact date every year—Easter, Ramadan, Chanukah, among many others—are not included.

A special note: religious observances can be unparalleled times for amplifying our ties to the past. Rituals foster connection. To increase their memory-preserving potential, though, you must talk about them. It's wonderful to color your Easter Eggs the same way every year. It's even better if friends and family know *why*.

65.

January
Resolve to Act

Make this the year to remember *intentionally*. Start by picking just one Forget Me Not from this book.

66.

February

Share Your Love Story. Tell Theirs.

February 14 provides a wonderful excuse to honor every type of love, not just the romantic kind. So, what made the relationship with your loved one so special? As Valentine's Day approaches, gather a few photos, handwritten notes, or cards and post them online. Share with others why this person meant so much to you.

67.

March

Grow a Memory Garden

In celebration of the first day of spring, pay a visit to your local nursery and buy your loved one's favorite herb, plant, or flower. If it isn't warm enough yet where you live, pick something from a seed and plant catalogue. Make Love Rocks (Forget Me Not #10) and sprinkle them in the soil. Grow a memory garden to remember those you've loved.

68.

April

Fortify the Earth

Plant a memorial tree in recognition of Earth Day. Use websites like www.nationalforests.org (benefitting the National Forest System) or www.worldlandtrust.org (protecting wildlife habitats worldwide). Saplings can also be planted locally, and towns across the country host ceremonies for Arbor Day. You can also plant a tree in your Memory Garden (Forget Me Not #67).

69.

May
Mother Yourself

Go to a gallery.

See a movie.

Get a massage.

Indulge.

On Mother's Day, take time to care for yourself.

70.

June
Celebrate Dad

Make a quilt out of neckties. If you're handy, do this yourself. If you're not (like me!), work with a company like The Gazebo (www.thegazebo. com), an online quilting shop I first wrote about in *Parentless Parents*.

After my father passed away, I gave The Gazebo a collection of my father's neckties. Within a few months, I had a handsome 3' x 3' wall hanging.

I love this quilt. Each colorful strip of silk and wool fabric reminds me of my dad—the afternoons when I visited his office after school, the night he took me to the ballet when we were on vacation, the countless times he and I met for dinner, just the two of us, after I graduated college—and now I can share these memories with my children. Over time, the quilt has become a family heirloom, one that takes on even greater significance every Father's Day.

71.

July
Celebrate Their Legacy

At your next July 4th barbeque, serve a dish you closely associate with loved ones or even ancestors. Appreciating family heritage can be a meaningful source of pride and remembrance.

72.

August

Plan a Connection Vacation

Visit the places where your loved one spent the most time. Talk with neighbors, friends, colleagues, and classmates. You'll likely hear unfamiliar stories and feel a fantastic sense of warmth and gratitude. To incorporate a digital component to this project, see Forget Me Not #40 on recording a digital walking tour.

73.

September
Recognize Every Grandparent

Every year, the Parentless Parents organization turns National Grand–parents Day into a magnificent opportunity to honor the grandparents who are no longer with us.

Proclaimed a day of observance by President Jimmy Carter and cel–ebrated the first Sunday after Labor Day, Grandparents Day recognizes the importance and influence of grandparents across the nation. While this remains the primary goal, many parentless parents have appropriated the occasion to build connection between children and their deceased grandparents.

Several Forget Me Nots are particularly well suited for Grandparents Day. The best activities include: Make a Frame (Forget Me Not #18), Create a Memory Magnet (Forget Me Not #19), or Stencil a Favorite Saying (Forget Me Not #51).

For additional ideas, please email me at allisongilbert@allisongilbert.com using "GRANDPARENTS DAY" in the subject line.

74.

October
Use Meaningful Halloween Decorations

Blogger Blair Stocker deserves all the credit for this Forget Me Not. Her Sinister Ceramics idea, as detailed in her book *Wise Craft: Turning Thrift Store Finds, Fabric Scraps, and Natural Objects into Stuff You Love*, fuels some of the best discussions I have with my children about their great-grandmother.

My grandmother Bertha joined a ceramics class when I was seven years old. In total she made more than a dozen pieces. Though many have broken over the years, I still have two—a perky kangaroo and a smiling Raggedy Ann doll. After my children outgrew them, I stored them in my basement, otherwise known as "heirloom purgatory." Until I read Stocker's book.

Stocker's Sinister Ceramics concept involves coating figurines such as cats, birds, and owls in black spray paint and sticking red jewels on the eyes. (I think Hummels work well, too, as they can be made to look especially creepy.)

I adore this project because it gives new life to old objects while simultaneously provoking conversation about the objects' origins. Giving Roo and Raggedy Ann a goth makeover gave me a chance to talk about my grandmother and reminded me of why she made them in the first place. Grandma Bertha sought out that ceramics class after my grandfather died and got out of it exactly what she needed—distraction, friendship, and a sense that she could be happy and engaged once again. Every figurine she made was proof of her resilience and grit. I tell this to my children every October, hoping to engrain in them the very attributes I admired in my grandmother.

For a while, I wondered what my grandmother would think of her ceramics' new, decidedly dark look. Would she be offended?

I truly don't think so. I like to imagine she'd be gratified I found a way to share a part of her life she was proud of, too.

75.

November
Honor Their Service

My friend Tanya Hunt has a framed letter in her house dated July 10, 1863. It's a precious family heirloom, written by her great-great-uncle just days after fighting for the Union army in the Battle of Gettysburg. And she's made certain her two teenage children know its history. "My husband and I always talk to our sons about relatives who served our country," she says. "It's an important reminder of why we have the freedom we enjoy."

On Veterans Day, use wartime memorabilia to honor loved ones who served. Pins, military papers, journals, and diaries all bolster reflection. Even if these materials have been displayed in your home for a long time, take advantage of the holiday to discuss their significance.

Very few objects in Tanya's house spark as much conversation as the imposing 4'3" wooden military musket (complete with 18" metal bayonet) that hangs above her fireplace. The gun belonged to her great-great-grandfather, who immigrated from Germany and settled on a farm near Sioux City, Iowa, in the early 1800s. Family lore says it was used in the Spanish-American War. "The rifle and Gettysburg letter are a part of us," Tanya reflects proudly. "If I don't talk about them, especially on Veterans Day, how could I expect my children to one day teach their children and pass these stories along?"

76.

November
Cook Together

There is no other dessert I associate more with my mother than her Fruit Platter Pie. And while serving it to my kids is always a treat for me, there's nothing better than making it *with them.* I use the extra time together to reinforce stories about their grandma. Jake and Lexi never met my mom, so these stories create memories my children would never have on their own.

Similar opportunities abound at Thanksgiving. Serving that special dish is great, but if you want to increase the chances of family and friends remembering why it's important to you, *include them in its creation.*

If you have hours to work with, present your youngest helpers with the recipe and ask them to write down the ingredients. When the shopping list is complete, bring children with you to the grocery store. I recognize it's nearly always faster to forgo this kind of help, but if you're open to the assistance, you'll create a bonus pocket of time to discuss why that pumpkin pie really matters.

And as for the adults, don't assume they know the story behind those special serving dishes and table linens—tell them.

77.

December
Deck the Halls with . . . Spools of Thread

Better-purpose ordinary inherited objects into extraordinary Christmas ornaments. Colorful spools of thread can be hung singularly or in a group. Keys of various sizes can be linked together with pretty ribbon. Inexpensive necklaces can replace or augment tinsel.

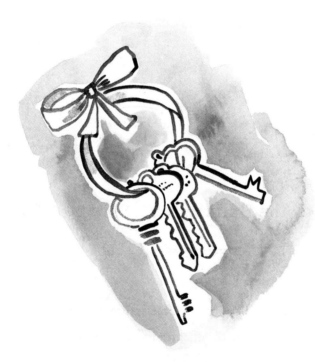

78.

December
Go Christmas Shopping

Buy a *new* ornament in memory of your loved one. Hang it on your tree.

5 *Places to Go*

Ecotourism. Adventure travel. Volunteer tourism. Specialized travel allows individuals and families to build entire trips around particular needs and interests—whether that be caring for endangered animals, jumping out of airplanes, or building schools in developing countries. Why not plan a vacation around honoring our connections to the past?

In 2014, author Hope Edelman and I customized an international experience for sixteen readers. The trip combined the physical challenge of hiking the Andes and Machu Picchu with an opportunity to help neglected and orphaned children. We called the expedition Turning Loss into Service: Motherless Daughters and Parentless Parents Unite to Help Orphans in Peru, and organized it with the help of Trekking for Kids, a nonprofit based in Washington, DC. The adventure accomplished exactly what we intended it to: a group of strangers, linked only by loss, came together for adventure, sisterhood, and an unmatched way to honor their mothers and fathers.

What do you call a trip that speaks to the desire to celebrate loved ones in the company of like-minded people? Let's call it Commemorative Travel.

The Forget Me Nots in this section stretch across three continents and seven countries. The destinations take you to diverse communities as far away as China, Japan, Israel, The Bahamas, Mexico, and Spain. They put you in the middle of national holidays and cultural events created largely around one purpose: remembering loved ones. They also bring you to iconic landmarks that are purpose-built for meaningful and spiritual connection.

If you can't picture this kind of travel in your immediate future, there's a very good chance you can find places to mark these international events in a town or city near you. Groups around the country, and some museums as well, host traditional celebrations like some included here. Of course, you can also cherry-pick aspects of these traditions and use them in whatever way speaks to you. With this in mind, each of the following Forget Me Nots is paired with opportunities to "Bring it Home," by which you can find these additional locations and ways to use rich and foreign customs to inspire your own practices and celebrations.

If you do consider traveling abroad to experience the occasions and places outlined on the following pages, Katherine Ashenburg, author of *The Mourner's Dance: What We Do When People Die*, an exquisitely researched book about loss and grief traditions around the world, says you shouldn't let language barriers deter you. "The desire to remember requires no discussion," Ashenburg told me. "You don't have to say or speak a word to understand that universal urge. The customs tourists see are also astonishingly visual, so there's really no need for interpretation." Ashenburg was moved to write the book after the sudden death of her daughter's fiancé; I highly recommend it.

More opportunities for Commemorative Travel exist than I can reasonably fit here. For additional ideas, please email me at allisongilbert@allisongilbert.com using "MORE TRAVEL IDEAS" in the subject line. I'll send you a list with bonus suggestions.

79.

Japan

OBON

One of the most spectacular rituals you'll see during Obon happens at the end of this deeply moving three-day festival. Thousands of candlelit lanterns are set adrift onto rivers and lakes across the country. It's believed the spirits of the dead return home during Obon; when the celebration ends, the flames guide them back to the afterlife.

Obon takes place during the summer, making it a wonderful addition to a vacation. While it is a time to honor the dead, it is not a wholly sad occasion: there are street fairs, carnivals, and plenty of traditional music and dancing. I first learned about Obon from reading Ashenburg's *The Mourner's Dance*, which offers a great deal of additional information and detail.

If you're thinking about making a trip to Japan during Obon, a great destination to consider is Kyoto, where, on the last day of the festival, five giant bonfires are lit on mountains surrounding the city.

BRING IT HOME

The easiest Obon-inspired activity you can do is to light several floating votive candles in memory of your loved one. This can be done anytime—all you need are appropriate containers and candles, both available online and in bulk.

If you're up for a domestic trip that takes the spectacle of Obon to another level, consider the following two options—one in Florida, the other in Hawaii.

Morikami Lantern Festival

Even though Obon is celebrated during the summer in Japan, the Morikami Museum and Japanese Gardens in Delray Beach, Florida, puts on an Obon-inspired Lantern Festival every fall, when the weather is more hospitable.

The Lantern Festival has gotten so popular that tickets must be purchased in advance. It boasts Japanese folk dancing, drumming, and garden paths lined with vendors selling traditional food and crafts. There's also mask-making and other activities for children.

The highlight of the day, of course, happens when it gets dark—when museum volunteers set aflame hundreds of floating paper lanterns they then gently push into Morikami's lake. For guests who have experienced loss within the last year, there's also the opportunity to purchase *tanzaku*, colorful strips of paper used for writing messages to loved ones. Guests place their handwritten notes into a large boat, which is set on fire during the ceremony, the smoke symbolically transporting the deceased to the next world for the first time. Visitors who buy paper lanterns can write messages on those, too.

For more details visit Morikami's website at: www.morikami.org/lanternfest.

Lantern Floating Hawaii

Every year on Memorial Day, the island of Oahu welcomes more than forty thousand people for Lantern Floating Hawaii. Started in 1999, this massive gathering began as a means of introducing Americans to the Japanese custom of floating paper lanterns. Organizers say Memorial Day was chosen because Americans were already in the mindset of honoring their dead. Today, the official website for the event says the celebration is a chance for anyone who has ever lost a loved one to "be surrounded by the love, understanding, and support of others—even strangers."

On the morning of the ceremony, participants collect materials to assemble a lantern at the Lantern Request Tent. Each lantern has three sides for writing messages of remembrance. Each family personally places their lantern into the water during the service. Because the observance takes place at night, the water gradually transforms into a sparkling and bobbing oasis of memories.

If you can't get to Lantern Floating Hawaii in person, you can submit a message online; it will be included on a Collective Remembrance Lantern during the ceremony.

For more information, visit: www.lanternfloatinghawaii.com.

80.

China

QINGMING FESTIVAL

Qingming Festival, or Tomb Sweeping Day, which typically begins April 4 or 5th, is a time for families to reunite and tidy the graves of ancestors—just as they have done for more than one thousand years. After paying their respects, many take advantage of the spring weather, indulging in picnics, going for walks, and flying kites.

Being a national holiday, Qingming is not a small, inconsequential occasion. Schools and offices are closed, and roads and cemeteries are packed. If you want to experience it as well, the best destination might be Beijing, where there are nearly 200 cemeteries.

Numerous travel websites have information about Qingming. I particularly recommend Dan Levin's 2013 *New York Times* piece "Festival's Resurgence Has Chinese Sending Manna to the Heavens," as it provides terrific background and overview (www.nytimes.com/2013/04/05/world/asia/in-china-a-newfound-interest-in-keeping-dead-relatives-happy.html).

BRING IT HOME

I like to think of Qingming as the Thanksgiving of memory-keeping.

Use the anniversary of your loved one's death as an excuse to get together with family. For this to happen, a fair amount of planning is required. You'll have to let relatives know what you have in mind and ask everyone to set aside sufficient time for an extended and purposeful visit.

Start with an unrushed graveside memorial service. Each participant can read prepared remarks, speak extemporaneously, or recite a poem. Take along a bottle of sparkling wine or cider to toast his or her life.

If children are joining you, bring sheets of white paper and a box of crayons. Encourage kids to do tombstone rubbings. Not only will this keep them busy, it will also dispel some of the notion that cemeteries are frightening places. If your family is comfortable with the idea and cemetery rules permit, you could continue with a relaxed Qingming-style picnic.

Similar opportunities are possible if your loved one was cremated. Plan a day trip or vacation for the sole purpose of distributing their ashes. Choose a special spot. Once there, take time to linger.

The standard practices of visiting cemeteries and scattering ashes often allow for only bursts of reflection. By infusing these rituals with practices inspired by China's Qingming Festival, you're able to break from these more commonplace routines, making the celebration of your loved one the primary reason for getting together.

81.

Mexico

DÍA DE LOS MUERTOS

Día de los Muertos, or Day of the Dead, is celebrated in Mexico and throughout Latin America on November 1 and 2. Despite its name, the festival is fun-filled and family-friendly. Like the Chinese Qingming Festival in Forget Me Not #80, Día de los Muertos is a national holiday marked by an entire population breaking away from its normal routine to honor the dead. Communities host boisterous and vibrant parades; amusement parks put on extravagant events. And children eat all sorts of themed candy—skulls and coffins made out of sugar, and lollipops in the shape of skeletons.

There are reflective aspects to Día de los Muertos, too. Families routinely create small altars in their homes with offerings to those they've lost. Items vary, but generally include food, photos, and mementos. Large altars are often erected in parks and public squares.

When I went to Mexico to research Day of the Dead, I spent a bit of time at Xcaret (pronounced *Esh-kar-et*), a sprawling tourist attraction near Cancún. The park has an extensive Day of the Dead program that's interesting for adults and appropriate for children of all ages.

For more information about Xcaret please visit: www.xcaret.com.

BRING IT HOME

Even though Día de los Muertos is celebrated in November, you can easily incorporate its most popular and festive touches into your Halloween festivities.

Cover tables with traditional decor: candy skulls, mini skeletons, and brightly colored paper flowers. Party stores carry these decorations, including theme-ready banners and streamers.

To infuse the party with poignancy, encourage guests to bring a main dish or dessert reminiscent of their loved one. You can also ask them to bring a photo and brief story to share.

82.

Thailand

The floating lanterns of Japan's Obon tradition are also part of the Yi Peng Festival in Thailand—except that in this case thousands of paper lanterns are released into the night sky as well. The massive display of twinkling lights has been described as "spellbinding" and "breathtaking"—like a "massive swarm of fireflies taking off towards the moon."

Yi Peng is a massive celebration in Chiang Mai, a large city in the northern part of the country, and takes place in November (dates vary and are contingent on the lunar calendar). In Buddhist culture, the lighting of paper lanterns is symbolic of leaving behind sadness and welcoming a brighter future. The ritual is also meant to bring good luck. Upon releasing the lanterns, individuals make wishes, often in memory of loved ones.

One way to experience this jaw-dropping spectacle is to participate in the massive Lanna Dhutanka Sky Lantern Release in Maejo, which is about seventeen miles outside Chiang Mai. Before crowds arrive during the day, organizers arrange poles with paper lanterns attached on a large field. As is done for a giant outdoor concert, people pour onto the grounds as early as possible to choose their spot; by nightfall, the crowd is massive. Then, on the cue of organizers, a crowd of thousands—some estimates put the number at five thousand—simultaneously release their lanterns.

To learn more about the Sky Lantern Release in Maejo, check out www.thaizer.com, a website and blog written by Roy Cavanagh. For more about Yi Peng, visit www.fest300.com, a listing of the top three hundred festivals around the world.

One of the reasons Yi Peng and the Lanna Dhutanka Sky Lantern Release in Maejo are ideal for remembering is because watching a paper lantern float away after you've released it can feel cathartic and freeing—in a way, delivering your thoughts more directly to the person you miss most. In many parts of the world, though, local fire and other safety regulations would likely prohibit such an activity. And this is why I must tell you about RiSE.

The RiSE Festival puts on lantern release events in the Mojave Desert, Nevada. On its website (www.risefestival.com), there's a promotional blog post from Alisen Dupre, a young mom who lost her mother to breast cancer in 2011.

Dupre gave birth to her son, her first, just two weeks after her mother died, so her later RiSE experience was particularly meaningful to her. "Love filled the air," she wrote. "There was a feeling of hope and togetherness that all of our messages would be lifted up. The phone line I wanted all those years to use to communicate with my mom came in the form of a large white, crisp lantern."

RiSE organizers say they use only biodegradable lanterns and conduct a miles-wide, 72-hour clean up following the event to recover them. If Nevada is too far to travel, I recommend releasing a balloon instead, writing a message on it to your loved one in permanent marker. A biodegradable balloon without string is a great option to consider. Pick a spot free of trees and let it go.

83.

Israel

The Western Wall in Jerusalem is considered by many to be Judaism's most sacred place. It's also one of the most important cultural sites in the world, one where tourists of every nationality and faith engage in a private spiritual expression: writing a prayer on a piece of paper and tucking it in between the Wall's ancient stones.

It's estimated that more than one million notes are placed in the cracks and crevices of the Western Wall every year. The slips of paper contain messages asking for virtually anything—peace, love, health, forgiveness, and strength. Prayers can be for yourself or others. The custom of inserting written prayers is so popular that presidents Barack Obama, Bill Clinton, and George W. Bush have all visited the Wall, as have Madonna, Ashton Kutcher, Rihanna, and Pope Francis.

The Western Wall is open 24 hours a day, 365 days a year. It can also be visited virtually via *Jerusalem*—a documentary (in both 2-D and 3-D formats) distributed by National Geographic—which offers a sweeping overview of the Wall and the city's other religious sites, including the Church of the Holy Sepulchre and the Al-Aqsa Mosque.

BRING IT HOME

Much of the comfort derived from leaving a note at the Western Wall stems from the act of committing thoughts to paper. Instead of visitors just *thinking* about their deepest hopes or concerns, they *take action*.

The ability to do something, even just a small thing, contributes to a sense of satisfaction.

Psychotherapist Robert A. Neimeyer, a psychology professor at the University of Memphis, Tennessee, and author of *Techniques of Grief Therapy: Creative Practices for Counseling the Bereaved*, urges his colleagues to use various art forms in their work with the bereaved. Neimeyer prescribes drawing, collage, dance, music, and creative writing. About the latter he makes a special appeal: "Like other forms of expression," he explained to me, "writing helps us review, consolidate, and articulate our internal experiences. When we think about our loved ones, our ideas can be formless and vague. Thoughts can feel one-sided. When we write, our ideas undergo a sizeable transformation—and some of the dialogue we crave is restored."

From this standpoint, I encourage you to write one letter. At another time, whether spontaneously or on a special occasion or anniversary, write another. Neimeyer says the mechanics of writing—getting a piece of paper, finding a pen, devoting attention to the person we miss—converts our relationship from what seems intangible to one that's "substantial right now." To me, that really is the most essential point.

84.

The Bahamas

JUNKANOO IN NASSAU

Junkanoo (also known as Jonkonnu or Jankunu) is a mammoth cultural celebration that roars through many Caribbean countries. Perhaps its biggest, loudest, and grandest manifestation takes place in Nassau, capital of The Bahamas. There the Junkanoo parade winds through city streets throbbing with participants dancing, beating goatskin drums, playing trumpets and trombones—all wearing elaborate costumes and headdresses in a riot of feathers, finely cut pieces of paper, and colors. The parade takes place overnight twice every year: on December 26 (Boxing Day), and again on New Year's Day.

While the roots of Junkanoo are debated, it is largely viewed as being steeped in African tradition, having been kept alive—indeed, having flourished—on slave plantations in the eighteenth and nineteenth century. Kenneth Bilby, a former director at the Center for Black Music Research at Columbia College in Chicago, spent years on the ground in the Caribbean researching Junkanoo, taking a special interest in a few rural outposts in Jamaica where the tradition's original purpose hasn't been fully diluted by time. Bilby concluded that, while the festival today in many parts of Jamaica and The Bahamas is largely secular, the older versions he studied have "clear and incontestable spiritual meanings" and are "closely tied to rites venerating ancestors."

Today, Junkanoo is an adrenaline-charged expression of folk culture and a major tourist attraction. In fact, it's gotten so commercialized that the Bahamas National Festival Commission recently launched Bahamas Junkanoo Carnival, a series of concerts and parades that stretch across two islands and two months, from April to May. But, regardless of its mass-produced quality, the celebration is nonetheless a unique opportunity to honor the past in a grand, celebratory fashion.

To learn more about Junkanoo, visit www.bahamas.co.uk/about/junkanoo/what-is-junkanoo. The Carnival website is www.bahamasjunkanoocarnival.com.

BRING IT HOME

"Music," Kenneth Bilby told me, "is one of the strongest tethers we have to the past. It's a critically important carrier of memory."

Of course, you need not venture to the tropics to harness music's particular tether. To capture the connective power of music at home, crank up your iPod and dance to a favorite song. Sing a tune that made your loved one smile. Re-read Forget Me Not #56 (Listen to Music) and block out time to make a *meaningful* playlist to accompany your reminiscences or spark new ones.

85.

Spain

CAMINO DE SANTIAGO

Unlike the opportunities listed earlier in this section, it is unlikely you can fold the Camino de Santiago into a regular vacation. The Camino is a spiritual and physical journey winding mostly through Spain and a small section of France. It requires proper preparation, equipment, and a great deal of time and stamina. And while there are many routes, the longest taking 30–40 days and covering about 500 miles, all paths lead to Santiago de Compostela, a town in northwest Spain that was declared a World Heritage Site by UNESCO.

The Camino is a pilgrimage in every sense of the word—a chance for private reflection and prayer as well as for meeting travelers from around the world. The most popular path, which attracts more than 260,000 trekkers and bicyclists annually, runs through numerous villages and towns, crosses the Pyrenees, and passes by several rivers and valleys. Time on the Camino can be transformative. The potential for solitude allows the kind of uninterrupted time needed to reinvest in the relationship you've lost, while the ability to engage with others who are likely there for their own significant reasons presents an unrivaled context for developing new, meaningful friendships.

While it's fairly easy to get on and off the trail and there are no rules for how many miles have to be covered, many people travel the Camino for the satisfaction of receiving the Compostela, a certificate signifying completion of the pilgrimage. To earn the Compostela, travelers must cover the last 100 kilometers (a little more than 62 miles) of the Camino, along which they can get a piece of paper stamped as proof of having traversed that stretch.

The official website for the Pilgrim's Office in Santiago de Compostela is: www.peregrinossantiago.es. You can also learn more by visiting the city of Santiago de Compostela's tourist office at www.santiagoturismo.com/camino-de-santiago.

BRING IT HOME

Walking provides wonderful opportunities for reflection. But for time outside to be most beneficial, particularly for those of us who live in cities, it may be best to spend it in *nature.*

According to a 2015 study published in *Proceedings of the National Academy of Sciences*, individuals who spend time in green, natural spaces focus less attention on negative aspects of their lives and open themselves up to the kind of thinking that brings them joy.

Gretchen Daily, coauthor of the study, told me: "Never before have people been so detached from nature. At the same time, what we're seeing is a pronounced increase in anxiety and mood disorders, particularly among people in urban areas. There is growing evidence, however, that reintroducing nature to people who are deprived of it can improve mood. Many individuals feel better in a natural setting, perhaps because it helps them let go of pain."

Daily's study is far from the first to show the positive effects of nature on our brains. In Adam Alter's 2013 article for The Atlantic.com, "*How Nature Resets Our Minds and Bodies*," based on his book, *Drunk Tank Pink: And Other Unexpected Forces That Shape How We Think, Feel, and Behave*, the New York University professor argues the upside this way: "Nature restores mental functioning in the same way that food and water restore bodies. The business of everyday life—dodging traffic, making decisions and judgment calls, interacting with strangers—is depleting, and what man-made environments take away from us, nature gives back."

That's because, according to Alter, nature demands very little from us. We enjoy fresh air, warm breezes, the beauty of lakes, rivers and streams, all without having to give anything in return. Alter writes it's because of this stress-free association that those who spend time in nature have the chance to "think as much or as little" as they like. By removing stress, therefore, we increase the likelihood of contemplating what and *who* make us happy.

Creating this kind of positive space for remembering has been the backbone of every Forget Me Not in this book. It's also the springboard that enables us to celebrate loved ones who have *passed* while enthusiastically, unreservedly, and joyously embracing our *present.*

A Final Word of Encouragement

Eighty-five Forget Me Nots represent a lot of ideas for keeping memories of loved ones alive. And if you do the math, this book contains even more tips: the Places to Go chapter includes additional "Bring it Home" opportunities to help readers take advantage of concepts that derive from other countries and cultures.

Please do not let the volume of advice and guidelines keep you from using this handbook. Especially when loss is new, I recognize accomplishing anything, even planning what to eat for dinner, can feel overwhelming.

Be assured that, no matter how long it's been since you lost someone you dearly loved, none of the Forget Me Nots has to be done right now—or even this year. Try one or two. Do more later. After the initial sorting of my mother's possessions into "keep" and "donate" piles, it took me another fifteen years to use her handwritten recipes as framed art in my kitchen. Not only did I not have the brain space to consider such an idea when she died, such an easy project never would have crossed my mind. Martha Stewart I am not.

Increasingly, it's become clear to me that my search for ways to remember has been the single most essential factor in helping me heal from my losses. I've found peace because I've sought ways to stay connected. Being proactive *is* critical.

Let this book help you without judgment or stopwatch. It's here for you anytime, without pushing you, available to cheer you on in solidarity when you're ready.

Resources to Request

For more information about keeping memories of loved ones alive, please visit my website, www.allisongilbert.com. Here, I post ideas and strategies for celebrating those we miss most, as well as research and tips culled from other sources.

I've also created bonus resources about honoring connections to the past. You can request one or all by emailing me at allisongilbert@allison gilbert.com. The below documents are the ones I've referenced in *Passed and Present*:

- A list of additional Commemorative Travel opportunities. Please write "MORE TRAVEL IDEAS" in the subject line.

- A list of extra ways to delight in everyday and precious garments. Please write "MORE FABRIC IDEAS" in the subject line.

- A list of supplemental strategies to enhance your Grandparents Day celebration. Please write "GRANDPARENTS DAY" in the subject line.

You can also email me at allisongilbert@allisongilbert.com for information about preserving objects and heirlooms. By writing "PRESERVATION TIPS" in the subject line, I will email you best practices for ensuring books, film, 35mm slides, art, clothing and other sentimental possessions last as long as possible.

Opportunities to Connect

I've written two previous books about parent loss and how the absence of parents impacts the way mothers and fathers raise their own children. If these subjects interest you, you can join the Parentless Parents community page on Facebook, participate in a Parentless Parents support group across the United States or Canada; locations can be found on my website, www.allisongilbert.com, or email me at allisongilbert@allisongilbert.com for a copy of the "HOW TO START A PARENTLESS PARENTS CHAPTER" guide. This document is very helpful if no Parentless Parents support group currently exists where you live.

To share your tips and strategies for remembering loved ones, please join the conversation here:

- Facebook: facebook.com/agilbertwriter
- Twitter: @agilbertwriter
- LinkedIn: Linkedin.com/in/agilbertwriter
- YouTube: youtube.com/user/AllisonGilbertNY

- Instagram: @agilbertwriter
- Pinterest: pinterest.com/agilbertwriter

If you'd prefer to connect with me privately, you can always email me at allisongilbert@allisongilbert.com. I look forward to hearing from you.

Selected Sources

The first three words of each source below represent either the beginning of a written quote or reference to a complete work when the overall message is conveyed, not just a specific line of text. I have chosen not to include information readily accessible online or dates for interviews, workshops, focus groups, and email exchanges. If you're interested in these details, please reach out to me at allisongilbert@allisongilbert.com.

PREFACE

someone is missing: Elizabeth McCracken, *An Exact Replica of a Figment of My Imagination* (Little, Brown and Company: 2008), p. 184.

FOREWORD

Page xv *Kaplan's landmark book*: Louise J. Kaplan, *No Voice is Ever Wholly Lost: A Profound Exploration of the Experience of Separation and Loss and the Psychological Forces That Sustain the Dialogue Between Parents and Their Children* (Simon & Schuster: 1995).

Page xvi *since Motherless Daughters*: Hope Edelman, *Motherless Daughters: The Legacy of Loss* (Delta: 1994).

INTRODUCTION

Page xxiii *"One of the . . . "* Therese A. Rando, *How to Go On Living When Someone You Love Dies* (Lexington Books: 1988), p. 233.

"Keeping your loved . . . " Ibid., p. 232.

theory about it: J. William Worden, *Grief Counseling and Grief Therapy: A Handbook for the Mental Health Practitioner* (Springer Publishing Company, Third Edition: 2002).

Page xxiv *the landmark book:* Dennis Klass, Phyllis R. Silverman, Steven L. Nickman, *Continuing Bonds: New Understandings of Grief* (Taylor & Francis, 1996).

Page xxvii *Angelina Jolie wore:* Mary Green, "How Angelina Jolie Honored Her Mom at Her Wedding" (*People,* September 2, 2014).

anchor Robin Roberts: Bill Carter, "The Early Shift" (*The New York Times,* December 28, 2014).

Page xxviii *Rosanne Cash, now:* Emily Spivack, *Worn Stories* (Princeton Architectural Press: 2014), p. 25.

"The last time . . . " Arianna Huffington, "The End of a Grand Adventure" (Arianna Online, September 14, 2000).

CHAPTER 1: REPURPOSE WITH PURPOSE

Forget Me Not #1: Preserve Memories in Perpetuity

National Geographic magazine: Catherine Zuckerman, "Alternative Rock" (*National Geographic,* December 2014).

Forget Me Not #2: A Different Kind of Scrapbook

In her book: Jessica Helfand, *Scrapbooks: An American* History (Yale University Press: 2008), p. xvii.

Forget Me Not #5 Cultivate a Shrine

"Glean more happiness . . . " Gretchen Rubin, *Happier at Home: Kiss More, Jump More, Abandon a Project, Read Samuel Johnson, and My Other Experiments in the Practice of Everyday Life* (Crown Archetype: 2012), p. 22.

"In a little used . . . " Ibid., p. 33-34.

Forget Me Not #10 Give Fabrics New Life

"The best thing . . . " Marcie Chambers Cuff, *This Book Was a Tree: Ideas, Adventures, and Inspiration for Rediscovering the Natural World* (Perigee: 2014), p. 139.

Forget Me Not #11 Tell Stories One Stitch at a Time

"a way of . . . " Rebecca Ringquist, *Rebecca Ringquist's Embroidery Workshops: A Bend-the-Rules Primer* (Stewart, Tabori & Chang: 2015), p. 82.

Forget Me Not #18 Make a Frame

inspired projects found: Joe Rhatigan, *The Decorated Frame: 45 Picture-Perfect Projects* (Lark Books: 2002), p. 24-25.

"emotionally significant events . . . " James L. McGaugh, *Memory and Emotion: The Making of Lasting Memories* (Columbia University Press: 2003), p. 90.

Forget Me Not #19 Create a Memory Magnet

A 2013 CBS: "Pulse: Most Americans Have Refrigerator Magnets" (cbsnews.com, June 9, 2013).

and coauthor of, Life at Home in the Twenty-First Century: 32 Families Open Their Doors (The Cotsen Institute of Archaeology Press: 2012).

Forget Me Not #23 Reconsider Your Reflection

"A mirror can . . . " Anne Burt and Christina Baker Kline, *About Face: Women Write About What They See When They Look in the Mirror* (Seal Press: 2008), p. 7.

"what is naturally . . . " Ibid., p. 8.

"traveled an ocean . . . " Ibid., p. 61.

CHAPTER 2: USE TECHNOLOGY

Forget Me Not #31 Digitize Family Recipes and Make Them an Indelible Part of Your Life

"I came to . . . " Jonathan Safran Foer, *Eating Animals* (Little, Brown and Company: 2009), p. 11-12.

Forget Me Not #36 Hang On to Meaningful Posts and Emails

"When I reread . . . " Brian Stelter, "David Carr's 'Lasting Totem'" (modernloss.com, June 18, 2015).

Forget Me Not #39 Fabricate History

"lifelong dream of . . . " Stephanie Rich, *A Followed Path: Travels with My Grandfather* (Stephanie P. Rich: 2010), p. 5.

"an incredibly important . . . " Ibid., p. 154.

"was the closest . . . " Ibid., p. 5.

CHAPTER 3: NOT JUST HOLIDAYS

Forget Me Not #45 Build a Refuge

At the rising, Sylvan Kamens and Jack Riemer, "We Remember Them," *New Mahzor* (The Prayer Book Press of Media Judaica: 1977-78), p. 572.

Forget Me Not #48 Cook Grilled Cheese and Spaghetti

"Fire and knives . . . " Gwyneth Paltrow, *My Father's Daughter: Delicious, Easy Recipes Celebrating Family & Togetherness* (Grand Central Life & Style: 2011), p. 19.

"I always feel..." Ibid., p.12.

Forget Me Not #49 Work with a Medium

Left her "doubtful" Lisa Miller, *Heaven: Our Enduring Fascination With the Afterlife* (HarperCollins: 2010), p. 206.

"The beliefs I..." Claire Bidwell Smith, *After This: When Life Is Over, Where Do We Go?* (Avery: 2015), p. 205.

"very worthwhile" in... Ibid., p. 187.

"finding ways, no..." Ibid., p. 125.

Forget Me Not #60 Establish a New Spring Ritual

One version can, Eleanor Bourne, *Heritage of Flowers* (G.P. Putnam's Sons: 1980), p. 20.

CHAPTER 4: MONTHLY GUIDE

Forget Me Not #74 Use Meaningful Halloween Decorations

All the credit, Blair Stocker, *Wise Craft: Turning Thrift Store Finds, Fabric Scraps, and Natural Objects into Stuff You Love* (Running Press: 2014), p. 104-105.

CHAPTER 5: PLACES TO GO

Forget Me Not #79 Japan/Obon

I first learned, Katherine Ashenburg, *The Mourner's Dance: What We Do When People Die* (North Point Press: 2002).

Forget Me Not #80 China/Qingming Festival

Tomb Sweeping Day, Dan Levin, "Festival's Resurgence Has Chinese Sending Manna to the Heavens" (*The New York Times,* April 4, 2013).

one thousand years, Sarah Kramer, "Paying Respect To Ancestors" (*The New York Times,* April 7, 2013).

nearly 200 cemeteries, ("Cemeteries in Beijing Increased to 184, 3.5 Million People Expected to Sweep Tomb in Qingming" (China News Service [translated from Chinese], March 26, 2015).

Forget Me Not #83 Israel/Western Wall, Jerusalem

and author of, Robert A. Neimeyer, *Techniques of Grief Therapy: Creative Practices for Counseling the Bereaved* (Routledge: 2012).

Forget Me Not #84 The Bahamas/Junkanoo in Nassau

While the roots, Kenneth Bilby, "Surviving Secularization: Masking the Spirit in the Jankunu (John Canoe) Festivals of the Caribbean" (New West Indian Guide, Vol. 84 (no. 3-4): p. 179-223, (2010). Also see: "Masking the Spirit in the South Atlantic World: Jankunu's Partially-Hidden History" (Proceedings of the Ninth Annual Gilder Lehrman Center International Conference at Yale University: 2007).

Forget Me Not #85 Spain/Camino de Santiago

The Camino is, Sergi Ramis, *Camino de Santiago: The ancient Way of Saint James pilgrimage route from the French Pyrenees to Santiago de Compostela* (Aurum Press: revised and updated 2014).

According to a: GN Bratman, JP Hamilton, K Hahn, GC Daily, and JJ Gross, "Nature Experience Reduces Rumination and Subgenual Prefrontal Cortex Activation," (Proceedings of the National Academy of Sciences USA, Vol. 112 (no. 28): p. 8567-8572, (2015). Also see: GN Bratman, GC Daily, BJ Levy, and JJ Gross, "The Benefits of Nature Experience: Improved Affect and Cognition," (Landscape and Urban Planning, Vol. 138, p. 41-50, (2015).

"Nature restores mental . . . " Adam Alter, "How Nature Resets Our Minds and Bodies," (theatlantic.com, March 29, 2013.)

Acknowledgments

Like giving birth and eating, no human experience is more ubiquitous than dying, yet in all the research I'd done to the point of writing this book, remembering was always given short shrift in book stores. Pregnancy and parenting books, weight loss manifestos, and cookbooks are wildly popular because they tap into universal challenges and opportunities. They're nearly always upbeat and hardly ever taxing on readers. My goal from the outset was to make celebrating deceased loved ones just as inviting, fun, and accessible.

Laura Mazer, executive editor at Seal Press, understood and championed this vision from our first conversation. Her enthusiasm was matched by her ability to sharpen my focus and overall approach. Laura also partnered with me early on to make this book look and feel the way I envisioned it, agreeing to consider working with Jennifer Orkin Lewis and allowing me an atypical level of author input into the cover design and interior illustrations. For all of this and more, I am one very lucky author, and I am thrilled to again work with such a high-caliber and celebrated publishing house as Seal. For that, I also extend my sincerest thanks to Krista Lyons (publisher) and Donna Galassi (vice president and associate publisher) for so quickly and heartily embracing my homecoming. I offer special kudos to associate publicist Jesse Wentworth for reconnecting Laura and me, and my sincerest thanks to the PR and marketing team—Eva Zimmerman, Anna Gallagher, Sarah Juckniess, Ashley Redfield, and Emi Battaglia—for shepherding *Passed and Present* into the world. My sincerest thanks to Kirsten Janene-Nelson for her thoughtful treatment of this manuscript.

Passed and Present would not be in your hands without my agent Richard Morris at Janklow & Nesbit, who understood more than anyone the void this book would fill. Richard: You are not only a tireless supporter of my work; you are a prized and tough editor. Thank you for everything, always.

When I was beginning to seriously tackle this project, author Hope Edelman and I were leading the first Motherless Daughters and Parentless Parents trekking expedition. So it was then that I enjoyed very early brainstorming sessions with her over coffee in a tiny café in

Cusco, Peru. Such a dear and generous friend, she offered enthusiasm, wonderful suggestions, and leads for interviews. And then she honored me by agreeing to write the foreword. Hope: your counsel and wisdom are always astounding. There's also nobody I'd rather share a tent with at 13,500 feet. I can't wait for our next adventure.

Heartfelt thanks go to Jennifer Orkin Lewis. I had long been an admirer of Jennifer's work, and asked her to paint the illustrations even before my contract with Seal Press was signed. That's not to say we knew exactly what they'd be or how they'd look. For those decisions, Jennifer, Laura, and I regularly talked on the phone and emailed concepts back and forth. Jennifer nimbly straddled two competing demands on her time—offering her expertise and graciously welcoming feedback.

Jennifer also spoiled me by suggesting hidden opportunities to acknowledge the people I miss most. My grandmother and mother's favorite number was 26, so you'll see that number on the ticket stub in the painting that opens the Repurpose with Purpose chapter. We used my mother's name, Lynn, to illustrate Forget Me Not #28, and my father's name, Sidney, is the name on the letter tacked to the bulletin board for the opening illustration for the Monthly Guide chapter. And it's because of Jennifer's ingenious idea that I sprinkled other covert recognitions of my loved ones throughout the text. Since for a long time my aunt Ronnie lived in Santa Fe, New Mexico, I picked her name and the location for Forget Me Not #17. And you'll find my grandfather's nickname, Willie, within Forget Me Not #39. Jennifer: Thank you for your extraordinary kindness and generosity, but most of all, your talent.

I benefited immeasurably from a multi-hour focus group. Participants included Fiona Galloway, Tanya Monier (www.the-happy-badger.blogspot. com), Heather Reid (www.consigntrilogy.com), and Jenifer Ross (www. watercoolerhub.com). Thank you so much for your time and fantastic ideas. Pia Salk and Michele Firpo-Cappiello (www.found123main.org), Krista Madsen (www.sleepyhollowink.com), and Sheri Silver (www.sherisilver. com) also deserve my sincere appreciation for their energy and suggestions.

The genesis of Forget Me Not #26 is directly attributable to information gathered from several experts in the field of speech technology. Murray Spiegel, director of Applied Communication Sciences, a leader in the communications field with origins in Bell Laboratories, was a tireless partner in my search for ways to preserve a loved one's voice. Murray not only helped me understand the complex technological landscape of speech technology, he also helped me gather important information from his esteemed colleagues, who work in multiple labs, hospitals, and corporations across the country. The following men and women were exceptionally generous with their time: Sara Basson, Bruce Balentine, Charlie Judice, Jonathan Pearl, Roberto Pieraccini, and Nava Shaked. I also had important discussions with CereProc, an industry pioneer in Edinburgh, Scotland. I offer my profound gratitude to Tim Bunnell, director of the Center for Pediatric Auditory and Speech Sciences and head of the Speech Research Lab at Nemours/Alfred I. duPont Hospital for Children in Delaware, for spending many more minutes with me on the phone than he'd planned.

Wholehearted thanks go to all the esteemed experts, artists, and craftspeople I've highlighted. Your knowledge shaped many pages of this book, and I'd never have been able to imagine such fascinating ways to remember, honor, and celebrate loved ones without you. I also learned a tremendous amount from readers. Thank you for trusting me with your ideas so others could learn from them.

I offer special thanks to Patricia Corcoran, director of the Centre for Environment and Sustainability at the University of Western

Ontario and Captain Charles Moore, resesarch director at Algalita, for patiently explaining their work studying and naming plastiglomerates; Kelli Montgomery, director of the MISS Foundation; Emily Brewster, founder of Emily Jane Designs; Jessica Williams, co-owner of Brent & Jess; Dan Hill, founder of RiSE Festival, and Robert LoMonaco, owner of The Gazebo. Gabrielle Birkner and Rebecca Soffer are due particular recognition for their pioneering website www.ModernLoss.com. Gabi and Rebecca: your platform is validation and proof that there is a need and an appetite for candid conversations about grief.

Rabbi Michael Rascoe is also due special recognition. His efforts tracking down the first known publication of *We Remember Them* were essential to giving Rabbis Sylvan Kamens and Jack Riemer the credit they both deserve for writing such a magnificent and enduring poem. Deepest thanks, also, to Rabbi Kamens for being so very generous with his time. Rabbi Kamens: what an honor it was to connect with you during the course of writing of this book.

Martie McNabb and her Show & Tales would likely not have been included if it weren't for Ann Schaffer and Linda Coffin of the Association of Personal Historians. The opportunity to write about

Legacy Republic comes first from Laura Murray and followed by representative Kris LeDonne, who eagerly shared her expertise with a group of enthusiastic testers, myself included. And thank you to all the public relations, marketing professionals, and assistants who facilitated the flow of information for this book: Monika Amar, Matthew Deighton, Charlene Flanter, Susan Glasier, Nikki Lowry, Molly O'Connor, Monica Rowe, Cathy Seehuetter, Chanel Williams, Deb Jordan, Marie Larson, Taylor Lavender, Shandi Kano, and Paula High.

For their assistance researching and fact-checking, my thanks go to Drew Bernstein, Phoebe Forlenza, and Ames Tardio. For translating numerous articles in Chinese newspapers into English for Forget Me Not #80, I offer my appreciation to Stanley Ip and Adam Wu. For enabling me to learn even more about the Qingming Festival I thank Dan Levin of *The New York Times*, who graciously aided me from his perch in Beijing. And utmost thanks go to my friend and *New York Times* international editor Greg Winter for connecting us.

My gratitude also extends around the world to Tawalan Sookying, Kedsarin Hasenfus, Batya Davis, Roscoe Dames, and Arlene Ferguson for strengthening my understanding of traditions in Thailand, Israel, and The Bahamas. I am also appreciative of the help provided to me by Alvaro Visiers in the Tourist Office of Spain.

I also offer my appreciation to Janet Roberts and Joy Johnson of Centering Corporation and Les Morgan of Growth House. Your unique capacity to investigate the landscape of existing bereavement literature gave me the confidence I needed to move forward. And for providing both access to a countless supply of books and the perfect study spot—a tiny wooden table nestled in the stacks underneath an arch of exposed bricks— my profound gratitude goes to everyone at the Irvington Public Library in Irvington, New York, including Rosemarie Gatzek (director), Pamela Bernstein (assistant director), and the finest reference staff around: Daniel Dibbern, Steve Fondiller, and Mindy Gordon.

Thanks go to my friends Betsy Cadel (for being a sorcerer with words), Tanya Hunt (for sharing your family's story with me and always having my back), Kristin Brandt (for painstakingly combing through early drafts of this book and offering critical edits), Gretchen Rubin and Kamy Wicoff (for helping me make tough decisions), and Tracy Costigan and Janet Rossbach (for a lifetime of laughs and friendship).

For their unwavering support and affection, Marilyn Weintraub, Jim and Sandy Weintraub, Cheryl Gilbert, and Jay Gilbert. I love you.

To my husband, Mark Weintraub: the publication of this book coincides with our twentieth year of marriage. I don't think there's any greater expression of my adoration for you except to say I'd do it all over again. We met as teenagers and have grown with each other ever since. You were my crush, and you'll always be my soul mate.

To my children, Jake and Lexi: I've come to recognize that one of the most powerful statements parents can make about their children centers on the pride they feel when thinking and talking about them. *Both of you make me so proud to be your mom.* I love you very much, and I can't wait to see where all your gifts and passions take you.

And, finally, to the family I've lost:

my mother, Lynn Tendler Bignell,

my father, Sidney Philip Gilbert,

my aunt, Ronnie Tendler Brachman,

my uncle, Richard Gilbert,

my grandmother, Bertha Gilbert,

and my grandfather, William Gilbert:

I miss you and often bring you up in conversation. And by writing about you in this book, including a few clandestine nods in the illustrations and text, I am keeping your memory alive. You may have passed away, but you are very much part of my present.

About the Author

© Elena Seibert Photography

Allison Gilbert is the author of *Parentless Parents: How the Loss of Our Mothers and Fathers Impacts the Way We Raise Our Children* and *Always Too Soon: Voices of Support for Those Who Have Lost Both Parents.* An Emmy award-winning journalist, Gilbert is also co-editor of *Covering Catastrophe: Broadcast Journalists Report September 11,* the definitive historical record of how broadcast journalists covered that tragic day. The groundbreaking book was turned into a documentary by the U.S. State Department and distributed to embassies and consulates around the world.

Nearly killed on September 11 reporting the news, the emergency triage tag put around Gilbert's neck is on display at the 9/11 Memorial Museum. Gilbert is also the only female journalist to be featured in the museum's official audio tour, her voice and story introduced by Robert DeNiro.

Gilbert's reporting has been honored by the National Academy of Television Arts and Sciences, the Associated Press, and the Society of Professional Journalists. For *Parentless Parents*, she is also winner of the Washington Irving Book Award. Gilbert and her work have been featured in *The New York Times, The Atlantic*, and The Huffington Post, and on NPR, CNN, FOX, MSNBC, CBS, and ABC.

www.allisongilbert.com
Facebook: facebook.com/agilbertwriter
Twitter: @agilbertwriter
LinkedIn: Linkedin.com/in/agilbertwriter
YouTube: youtube.com/user/AllisonGilbertNY
Instagram: @agilbertwriter
Pinterest: pinterest.com/agilbertwriter

Selected Titles from Seal Press

We Hope You Like This Song: An Over Honest Story about Friendship, Death, and Mix Tapes, by Bree Housley. $16.00, 978-1-58005-431-7. Sweet, poignant, and yet somehow laugh-out-loud funny, *We Hope You Like This Song* is a touching story of love, loss, and the honoring of a friendship after it's gone.

1,000 Mitzvahs: How Small Acts of Kindness Can Heal, Inspire, and Change Your Life, by Linda Cohen. $16, 978-1-58005-365-5. *1,000 Mitzvahs* shares Cohen's two-and-a-half-year journey from sorrow to inspiration through simple daily acts of kindness. The myriad forms they take—from helping the elderly to donating to good causes to baking and collecting food for others—highlight the many ways in which one person can touch the lives of others and enhance her own well-being.

All the Things We Never Knew: Chasing the Chaos of Mental Illness, by Sheila Hamilton, $24, 978-1-58005-584-0. *All the Things We Never Knew* takes readers on a breathtaking journey from David and Sheila's romance through the last three months of their life together as David's bipolar disorder pulled their lives apart and into the year after his death. It details their unsettling spiral from their lives before his illness and reveals the true power of love and forgiveness.

Under This Beautiful Dome: A Senator, A Journalist, and the Politics of Gay Love in America, by Terry Mutchler. $17.00, 978-1-58005-508-6. *Under This Beautiful Dome* tells the true story of journalist Terry Mutchler's secret five-year relationship with Penny Severns, an Illinois State Senator who mentored Barack Obama. Denied legal access to the altar, they face even greater hardships when Penny is diagnosed with cancer and begins undergoing treatment. This vivid, beautiful story paints an intimate portrait of a loving relationship and the vast impact gay marriage legislation has on couples and families in America today.

Shades of Blue: Writers on Depression, Suicide, and Feeling Blue, by Amy Ferris. $16.00, 978-1-58005-595-6. The silent epidemic of depression affects millions of people and takes dozens of lives everyday, while our culture grapples with a stigma against open discussion of mental health issues. Editor Amy Ferris has collected these stories to illuminate the truth behind that stigma and offer compassion, solidarity, and hope for all those who have struggled with depression.

The Goodbye Year, by Nona Willis Aronowitz and Emma Bee Bernstein. $19.95, 978-1-58005-273-3.

Find Seal Press Online
www.SealPress.com
www.Facebook.com/SealPress
Twitter: @SealPress